Remember to Breathe
A story of second chance

Louise Ayden

A work of fiction
The moral right of the author has been asserted.
This is book is sold subject to the condition that it shall not, by way of trade or otherwise, be lent resold, hired out or otherwise circulated without the publisher's prior consent in any form of binding or cover other than that in which it is published.
Copyright © by Louise Ayden 2009
First print 2015
Revised version 2016
louiseayden@gmail.com

ISBN: 978-09809729-1-0

The only thing we never get enough of is, love.
And the one thing we never give enough of is love.
Henry Miller

Also by Louise Ayden
I Belong to Me

This novel is dedicated to
Sophie

1

A loud, ominous sound rumbled in the distance like cannon fire, as angry dark clouds crept across the steel-grey sky, snatching the last remnants of daylight. In the gloom, heaven opened and spewed down hail the size of tennis balls. Silver tentacles slithered across the sullen horizon for brief illuminating seconds, revealing eerie shadows clawing vortex bushland. The squall rose and fell, slapping the National Line's coach as its engine groaned under the strain of the steep McPherson Range climb, en route to Northern Queensland.

Ali Swanson swayed back and forth in rhythm with the vehicle as it struggled with the storm. She slept a less than peaceful sleep. Her eyes fluttering like butterflies wriggling from their cocoon about to embark on a whole new life, as snapshots of jitterbugging images lurked in her mind. Those restless eyes sprang open as a sudden violent jolt shook the coach as it hit the shoulder of the road.

"What the …" Ali yelled, bolting upwards, gripping the edge of her seat, ready to flee. Her heart thumped hard in her chest and tiny beads of sweat assembled along the edge of her top lip. She scanned her surroundings with wide-eyed terror but there was nothing sinister to harm her, just sleeping passengers rocking to and fro, and others shifting about in an effort to get comfortable – the scene eased the tension she felt. Her eyes met the driver's. He gave her a smile that said, 'Everything's ok.' She let go a long sigh and whispered the words, "remember to breathe."

Relaxing back into the seat, calm settled a little within her when she remembered that she was on a coach travelling north. 'Melbourne would be well and truly behind me by now,' she thought, but suspicion was still a close companion as recent events tumbled around in her mind. She bent down and lazily picked up her battered backpack off the floor and began rummaging through it for her mobile. She found it, flipped it open and glared contemptuously at the illuminated clock. *'Time,'* she thought, feeling at a loss, *'I've got plenty of that now; I just have to figure out what I'm going to do with it.'*

Ali left Melbourne without direction or a plan; the decision to leave was made on impulse being aware that she was the architect of her life, and that she had better reconstruct it and reset her compass or she would soon be extinct. Her lean, tortured body began to tremble. All that thinking had set off her nicotine craving. She cursed the hours left until the next stop – the void forced her to take stock of the tangled threads of her life.

2

The early morning sun streamed through Olivia Rossetti's bedroom window, sending a prism of colour around the room and across Olivia's face, as the rays caught the crystal vase sitting on the bedside table. She stirred and grudgingly forced her eyelids apart to stare squint-eyed at the clock. "Oh no," she moaned, irritated with herself, "damn! I've overslept."

Instead of getting up right away, as she should, Olivia reached over and turned on the radio. Then rebelliously rolled on to her stomach and buried her face deep into her pillow, fighting the urge to sleep on, even though the old clock radio was loud enough to wake the dead. *"The time is 5.45 am. Today looks promising. The sun is bidding us a good morning after that freakish storm yesterday afternoon ..."*

"Oh, shut up! How can you be so cheerful?" Olivia barked at the effervescent DJ resentfully tossing aside the bed covers and staggering half-asleep to the bathroom. As Olivia was about to step into the shower, she caught sight of her naked image in the full-length wall mirror and smiled, "You've still got it, kid," she proudly boasted, playfully flicking her dark shoulder-length hair. "A bit chubby perhaps, but that's ok. I'm not busting my tush off at the gym to appease anyone. I like you just the way you are," she confidently declared to her reflection, "and that's all that matters."

When dressed, Olivia did as she had done so many mornings over the years. She went to the kitchen, made a cup of coffee and took it to the lounge room where she sat in her favourite chair. Her large brown eyes softened when she gazed lovingly through the side window, at her herb garden, the garden that she and Anton had designed together, so long ago. Sage, rosemary, dill and mint blended perfectly with the other herbs. Their exotic scent drifted through the open window and into the room. Olivia closed her eyes and breathed in deeply, drawing in every precious memory of them planning and planting the herbs and shrubs, along with the scent.

They first met in kindergarten. "I'm going to marry, Olivia ..." Anton announced to his family, after his first day at kindy. Sixteen years later, he was waiting at the altar for his bride and, twelve months on, Ben, their only child was born.

Olivia was about to slump back in her chair and revel in bygone days, when the DJ announced the time again.

"Damn!" she exploded in mild frustration, jumping up. "There *never* seems to be enough time in the day."

On her way out, family photographs on the Chippendale sideboard that they bought at a local garage sale, caught her attention. Her eyes fell upon Ben and Julia's wedding photo. "We've all come a long way since that day my darlings," she told the photograph. As she smiled lovingly at their image, while holding the frame in both hands, Ben's voice echoed in her mind. He was telling her that Julia had confessed to him on the eve of their wedding, how she did not understand the close relationship he has with her, that she felt threatened by it. *'Mum, Jules' parents were too bloody busy building an empire to spend time with her as a child. She was raised by uncaring nannies and now she believes that if her parents didn't want her, why would anyone else?'*

Resolved to have a good relationship with Julia for Ben's sake, Olivia made every effort to understand her daughter-in-law's insecurities. *'Hmm, that reminds me,'* Olivia thought scratching around in her bag for her diary, *'I must call Julia to make a time for lunch.'* She glanced at her watch. "Bloody hell," she said, "I'll have a riot on my hands, if I don't get moving and open the café." But then, another distraction delayed her again. She could not resist picking up Anton's photo. She kissed it and said, "I love you, darling."

"I know, and I love you, go, go."

"Ok, ok, I'm gone."

3

The driver carefully navigated the cumbersome vehicle into the Corner Café's parking lot around 7.45am. As he wearily climbed out of his seat he trumpeted, "Wakey! Wakey everyone! We're stopping here for breakfast! This café has the best tucker in town …"

His husky voice effectively penetrated the brains of the stiff, dishevelled, clammy bodies as they stretched back to life, "… and you've got 30 minutes to get a meal, do what you have to do and get back on board. "Sorry, guys," he shrugged apologetically, "I can't wait for stragglers; I'm runnin' behind schedule because of the storm. This is an unscheduled stop because the highway's flooded …"

Before the driver finished talking, Ali had stood up, tossed her backpack over her thin shoulder and was edging her way to the exit. She slowly weaved her way through the maze of travel-weary passengers, stepping over luggage blocking the aisle. The pungent stench of stale air and body odour assaulted her nostrils. She hastened her steps, shoving some passengers aside. "Hey," someone yelled, "watch it," and she mumbled an ambivalent apology.

Relieved to finally inhale clean, fresh air, Ali stepped from the coach into a puddle, a remnant from the recent downpour. She was too awe-struck by the tropical splendour to care that her only footwear was soaked through, and did a quick 360 turn. Something vaguely familiar about the place heightened her pleasure about being there; *a snapshot of her and her brother as children playing at the shore's edge flashed into her mind, a pretty five-year old with bouncy, raven curls and huge lavender eyes, with a toddler, her brother, Billy. They were playing in the sand as her parents, Steven and Elizabeth Swanson, stood nearby, watching them. A shimmery, golden, hazy silhouette, standing a short distance from them, waved.* Laughter momentarily bounced around in her head and then suddenly stopped, as the images shattered into a million fragments and vanished.

Instead of following the other passengers into the café and getting something to eat, Ali lit up a menthol cigarette and drew back hard on it. She closed her eyes and lifted her face towards the sun. Through pursed lips, she pumped out smoke rings, one after the other into the air, and watched them float upwards and fade away. She dropped the cigarette then stubbed it out with the toe of her boot, and casually strolled off to look around. She came across a pathway that led her into a thick rainforest. Glimpses of an azure bay through the trees painted a scenic backdrop for the dozen or so holiday cabins sheltered under twelve-metre high, rough fern trees. The magical blended tapestry of jade, avocado, lime and emerald lulled her. Farther along, she spotted the local noticeboard with the village name written above it in large, bold lettering. *Hmmm, Segal Bay, huh? Never heard of it, 2000 residents, a seaside village. Hmm, tranquil and revitalising. Yep, that sounds good to me,'* she thought, as a plan began to form in her mind. Ali carefully read every notice on the board until she found something useful. A help wanted notice caught her attention. She snatched the handwritten note from the board. Her large, lavender eyes narrowed, weighing up the pros and cons of her situation. "That'd be right," she grumbled in frustration, as well as from sleep deprivation, "no freaking information, just a number."

4

Olivia struggled to disguise her surprise when the girl entered the café and asked to speak to the owner. "I'm Ali Swanson," she said, trying to sound more confident than she felt. "I called a few minutes ago about the job. I spoke to Olivia. She told me to come in, and see her. Ali paused then shrugged, "So I'm here."

Olivia's mind was racing, *'Oh my goodness! This isn't what I was expecting.'*

In an attempt to ease the awkwardness between them, Ali rambled on. "I was on my way up north with this lot," inclining her head toward the rowdy, scruffy passengers, wolfing down breakfast, "That was before I found your sign on the noticeboard, and thought, why not? I definitely need a change of scenery and this place seems perfect." Ali paused briefly, smiled warmly and said, "It's awesome!"

Olivia finally recovered. "Well yes, yes, Ali, you spoke to me. I'm Olivia."

"Hi," the girl replied a little awkwardly, clearly aware by Olivia's paralysed expression that she looked out of place.

"Umm, well, as you can see we're very busy at the moment. We can talk after the rush – ah, that's if you're not in a hurry to get the coach?"

"Nup," Ali shrugged, "I've got plenty of time, even told the driver not to wait for me." Pausing again, Ali did a quick

180 turn and pointed to a booth. "Mind if I wait over there by the window?"

Olivia seemed distracted, as though she had not heard what the girl said. Ali followed the direction of Olivia's eyes and thought she saw a man sitting in the booth she had chosen. But changed her mind, thinking it was just a reflection in the window when Olivia finally spoke. "Sure Ali, I'll be back soon," Olivia said, hurrying off to serve a customer.

The girl casually strolled over to the booth and sat down. Leaning back, she observed her surroundings with light-hearted amusement. Red vinyl booths, oscillating black-vinyl counter stools, black and white harlequin floor, booths covered in red vinyl and even a jukebox playing fifties and sixties music. Grinning to herself, she was thinking, *'S'pose the Fonz is the waiter.'*

The aroma of coffee, sizzling bacon and eggs, sausages and baking bread wafting through the room made her feel ravenous. She could not remember when she last ate a decent meal. It surprised her how much she liked the place and how at ease she felt, sitting there watching the hustle and bustle buzz around her; the murmuring of voices, spontaneous laughter and music from the juke box playing softly in the background, soothed her anxiety.

Suddenly, her inquisitive eyes shot towards the door. Two men dressed in black came in. One tall and wiry as a string bean and the other who looked older was short, stout and balding at the crown. She noticed that they both nodded to Olivia and the shorter man mouthed, "Our usual please," on their way to the booth adjacent to hers. The older man did a double-take when he saw Ali. Her eyes narrowed in suspicion when he whispered something to his friend and turned towards her. She quickly looked away. With several tiny steps, a hip wriggle, he was standing arms-folded, beside her. His disapproving stare unsettled her as every nerve in her body twitched. She wanted to run, but she was too afraid to move. So she pretended to ignore him and nervously flipped through the menu.

"Well," he finally said, "no one told me they were casting again."

"What?" Ali looked directly at him, confused. She was expecting a badge flashed and 20 questions.

"The way you are dressed, sweetheart, someone must be casting for the remake of *Romper Stomper*. Your *style* just won't do around here, baby girl. It's got to be a movie, hmmm?" He said, rubbing his chin. "No, no. Can't be that, I'd have known about it. So what are you doing here?"

Concerned that there would be trouble, Ali placed the menu on the table and slowly slid out of her booth and stood to face him. She seemed to tower over the intruder and looked very intimidating. She mustered up enough courage to ask, "Are you the law around here?"

"Aaah, no," the man replied a little warily. With a confidence rush, he squared up and proudly announced, like she should have known, "I am Jonathan Starr, the local hairstylist, AND f-a-s-h-i-o-n consultant; something of which you could use, quick time." He paused and looked over his shoulder and beckoned to his friend, who quickly joined them.

"This gorgeous man is Montague Harris, affectionately known as Harry; my life partner, and the other half of *Cut & Dry*, the best salon you'll ever enter, by appointment only." Jonathan Starr beamed.

Ali let out an enormous sigh and nearly fell backwards into the booth, struggling to stifle a belly laugh.

Olivia was keeping an eye on Ali from the kitchen. Her eyes widened with concern when she saw Jonathan standing over her. "Quick! Quick! Madison, make a short-black and flat-white for Jonathan and Harry, I'll take it over to them. Their meals are ready. "Oh dear!" Olivia mumbled to herself, "Looks like Ali needs rescuing." She looked totally confused when Ali stood up, "Perhaps it's the men who need rescuing."

"Here we go, breakfast." Olivia said smiling at her friends. 'I see you've already met Ali. She'll be helping out around here for a while."

The men glanced at one another. Their brows creased and then rose upwards as they responded in unison, "Really?"

"Yes," replied Olivia, giving them her *don't-give-me-a-hard-time* look.

The hairdressers went back to their booth and discussed Ali over breakfast. Glum-faced Jonathan rotated his head back and forth like a carnival clown, observing the stranger. "I don't know about this girl, Harry." Jonathan whispered, crinkling his brow deeper, "She looks like trouble to me."

"I'm not so sure," Harry whispered back, "By the look of those scars, especially the one around her throat. I'd say she's had a tough time."

"Nooo!" Jonathan gasped, utterly horrified. "I didn't even notice. Oh my God! I was distracted by her wardrobe. It's sooo awful and that *hair* – it's a paint palette gone wrong, but her eyes are *stunning*!"

Shaking his head, Harry flashed Jonathan a scathing look and Jonathan quickly apologised. "I can be such a cow at times. Sorry. We have to do something, Harry. She can't work here looking like that. That girl definitely needs a make-over, she looks trashy, oops, sorry, I mean, so she'll *blend in*."

Harry nodded and smiled warmly at Jonathan while thinking how frustrating he is. "That's a wonderful idea. We'll grab her when Livvy's finished the interview."

Ali sensed the men would probably be averse to her, and seriously considered moving on, but after talking to Olivia, she decided to take the job. She liked Olivia and there was something special about the café too. It felt safe.

"You can stay in one of the cabins until you find a place, in exchange for a few extra hours a week, ok?" Ali agreed. "Come on then, I'll show you around."

They walked just a few paces when Olivia stopped suddenly and turned to face Ali. "The coach doesn't stop here often, you know. So I am assuming that *fate* has brought you here. I hope that's a good thing, Ali."

"Ali!" Jonathan called and rushed over to her. "Aaaaah, umm," He stammered, "when you have a moment, will you come to our salon, pleeease? Olivia will show you where we are."

"Why?"

Harry jumped up from his seat and dashed over to Ali. "Because we want to apologise for being so rude to you, just come. We think you will like our apology."

Ali shrugged, "Maybe."

Olivia nodded and winked at them.

5

Olivia and Ali strolled down the path to the cabin in silence, the same path Ali wandered just a few hours before. Solar lights, resembling tiny soldiers in tin hats, flanked either side of the path all the way up to the cabins.

Both women were immersed in their own thoughts. Ali, although puzzled by Olivia's generosity, was very grateful for it. She was thinking about what her therapist had told her during the sessions at the rehabilitation centre. *'Always take your time, Ali, and remember to breathe, slowly in and out whenever you feel uncertain. It'll give you time to think. Never, never, react impulsively, that will only bring you trouble.'*

Olivia, still unsure of Ali, guided her off the path and up to a cabin. The dozen or so birds scrounging around the forest floor screeched loudly and took flight at the sound of footsteps on the cabin's front landing. The ruckus the birds made jolted Ali back to the present.

"Wow"! Ali exclaimed, with child-like delight. "This is awesome. Are those gorgeous yellow flowers on that tree over there orchids?"

Olivia's eyes darted to where Ali was pointing and nodded. "This was our little piece of heaven," she smiled, recalling the hours she and Anton put in to create it. "Ant," Olivia was about to reminisce, but stopped herself. "Oh, never mind," she said, "I'm sure you just want to get settled in."

Ali wasn't listening. She was too engrossed with her surroundings. "Wow," she whispered to herself twisting and turning every which-way, fascinated with the lush green vegetation, stunning orchids and rainbow lorikeets, the view of the bay and the smell of warm salty air.

When Olivia unlocked the door, slid it open and stepped inside, Ali snapped out of her reverie and quickly fell in line behind her. She was not surprised to find a bright and cheery open-plan, bed-sitter with all the mod cons. It reflected Olivia and the café.

Olivia dashed about the room, opening and shutting cupboards and drawers showing Ali where things were. When finished, she jotted down her mobile number and directions to the salon on a scribble pad she found in one of the kitchen drawers and handed it to Ali.

"Well then, I guess that's about it for now." Olivia said, laughing a little nervously. *'I hope you know what you're doing, Anton,'* Olivia thought as she handed Ali the keys. "If you need anything, just call."

Ali nodded her thanks and then Olivia was gone, leaving her standing in the middle of the room, staring at the open door. The outside sounds of geckos, birds and rustling trees suddenly seemed amplified. The noise pounded in her head as tears of gratitude, flowed freely down her cheeks. "Do I really deserve all of this?" She asked the empty room? "I'm such a train wreck: always messing up everything. I can't do it again, not this time, I just can't."

Outside, Olivia walked a few paces and then stopped behind a tall fern. Separating its wide, emerald spidery branches, she peered at Cabin 4. *'What on earth am I doing?'* She was *thinking, 'I know absolutely nothing about this girl, except that she looks as if she has fought the world and lost.'*

In frustration, Olivia's hands shot up to her head. She ran them through her hair, gripping handfuls, wanting to scream out loud. But sounds coming from inside the cabin silenced her thoughts. She turned her head sideways and could just hear Ali crying and what she was saying – a sudden penetrating regret encumbered her as Anton's words sounded clearly in her mind, *"Oh yes, my darling that very old saying, you can't judge a book by its cover, is perennial."* Olivia smiled in agreement and headed back to the café.

The cabin phone was ringing. Ali sniffed back her tears and pressed the heels of her hands hard against her eyes, then wiped her face on the hem of her tee-shirt as she hurried to answer it.

"Did I wake you?" The caller asked before Ali spoke.
"Who's this?"
"Do I really have to say?"
Silence.
"How about you freshen up and come to the salon?"
Still no response

As seconds ticked away, Ali could hear noises through the earpiece.
"Give me that."
"No!"
"Ssssh!"
A slap.
A high-pitched yelp.
The commotion sounded as if they were squabbling over who talked to her.

"Okay," she finally said, but the caller did not hear her, so Ali said it again, louder.

"Oh, oh, in an hour then," The caller said, "if that suits you?"

"I'll see you soon," she mimicked laughing and then was serious, "Oh and, ummm, thanks guys for the invite."

Ali took a few minutes to wander around her new home once more, taking in everything with profound appreciation. She spied her backpack on the chair, picked it up and shook all her possessions onto the bed. A few items of clothing, toiletries, mobile and strips of leather she used as jewellery tumbled out. Rummaging through the jumble, she selected what she needed and took them to the bathroom.

Olivia was dawdling back to the cafe, lost in her thoughts, but sprang to life and glanced at her watch the instant she heard Madison Weston, the weekend casual calling her from the top of the path. "The lunch crowd," Olivia muttered, and then ran the rest of the way.

"I was getting worried, Olivia." Madison said, as she watched Olivia regain her breath. "It's a packed house today. I guess everyone's tired of being cooped up for days on end because of the rain. Now they're able to get out and about..."

"Oh, I am too old for this," Olivia said, interrupting her. She was gripping her knees struggling to breathe, "I'm so unfit" she moaned. "Perhaps I should join the yoga group," she laughed awkwardly.

"Are you serious, Olivia?" Madison said, expressing surprise at the pessimistic comment. She had always admired Olivia for her tenacity of never being fazed by anything. Olivia was her rock. Madison studied her boss for a moment. "Olivia, is everything ok?"

Olivia looked up as if she was about to say something, she smiled at Maddison instead and straightened up. "Yep, it's all good," she said unconvincingly, "C'mon we'd better get inside."

Olivia was about to run again, but changed her mind. She pulled her mobile from her pocket, looked over at Madison and asked, "How busy are we?"

Madison raised her eyebrows and nodded, "Really busy."

"Hello, Jules. I was going to see if you were available to join me for lunch today," Olivia laughed, "but things aren't going as planned. I'm calling to see if you can help out – now?"

6

The boutiques, cafés, restaurants and other shops in the main street of the small pedestrianised fishing village were refurbished fishermen's cottages. All of them looked as if they had been planted in between enormous palms and shrubs. After the recent downpour, a bitter-sweet odour of rotting vegetation and frangipani hung heavily in the air.

Ali strolled down the busy street, following Olivia's written directions. Inquisitive stares from passing vacationers unsettled her. She felt out of place in paradise, whereas on the streets of Melbourne she was invisible. A little farther on, she spied the caravan park sign, beyond that through the palms and rain forest, the afternoon sun. The huge red-gold ball slowly slid behind distant rolling hills. The evening sky was an artist's canvas – awash with deep purple, pink, crimson and golden splatters across the horizon and in contrast, trees framing the shoreline became twilight silhouettes. Ali was spellbound by nature's ritual to the end of the day. She turned suddenly. A familiar voice from behind disturbed her enchantment.

"Oh! I'm so sorry Ali," Harry said in earnest, stepping backwards. "I didn't mean to startle you."

Before she could respond, Harry moved closer and said, looking past her, "It's gorgeous, isn't it?"

She nodded and turned back to the sunset.

"Someone up there knows exactly what they're doing," he said.

For a brief moment, they stood together in hushed reverence. Then Harry broke the spell and said, "C'mon," with a tone of authority, "Jonathan is waiting," and took Ali gently by the arm and led her urgently down the street and around the corner to Hudson House, the tallest building in the district. They walked up a flight of stairs and turned left at the top, and then walked a few paces and came face to face with a six foot poster of Jonathan holding a hairdryer and Harry scissors, standing back to back in a James Bond pose; *Cut & Dry* in bold lettering splashed across the print.

Jonathan, swollen with pride, waited impatiently beside the sign. "I'm so glad you came, Ali. Come, come in. Welcome to our magnificent salon, *Cut & Dry*." His eyes sparkled as he inhaled deeply, ready to take a bow, expecting her to gush, ooohs and aaahs, as did all his new clients. When Ali said nothing, Jonathan's smile slid from his face. The corners of his mouth slowly drooped as his inflated pride gradually dissolved. His shoulders slumped lower the longer she remained silent.

Harry was baffled by Ali's silence and quietly observed her from the other side of the room. He was also mystified by her odd expression as she looked around the salon. He had no way of knowing she was thinking the stunning boutique salon, in the middle of an out-of-the-way seaside village, was familiar, but she could not recall why. The salon was indeed impressive. Spotlighting above the silver-framed mirrors facing the Italian black leather chairs were so bright that they made the high-gloss wooden floor look like glass. The white marble double-sinks shone as brightly as lighthouse beacons under the lights. Ali roamed the room and stopped behind one of the leather chairs. Her eyes took in everything around her, even noticing how the lighting highlighted the more expensive products.

"You're from Melbourne, aren't you?" She asked casually running her hand over the chair, appreciating the quality of the leather.

The men glanced warily at each other, "Yes, we are," Harry replied. Jonathan was still sulking. "Why do you ask?"

"Oh, no reason," she shrugged. "The salon's nice; so I figured…huh…oh, nothing."

"Nice?" The men mouthed behind her back, screwing up their faces in horror. *"Thousands of dollars of interior design and she calls it, 'nice'."* Jonathan's eyes were popping, suppressing a scream.

Oblivious to their reaction, Ali strolled over to the marble bench where an open concertina case displayed a full range of cosmetics and skincare products, brushes and other equipment. She nonchalantly looked at the cosmetics, raised her brows and mumbled, "Hmmm, impressive."

Hearing that, Jonathan pulled himself together and dashed to her side.

"These are my tools," he said, sweeping a caressing gesture across the case. "I work sublime magic with them. Would you like me to show you?"

Ali hesitated a moment before she cautiously nodded. Jonathan clasped her arm and led her to the chair where Harry stood straight and tall, holding a black cape. His posture reminded her of a matador about to enter a bull ring. She would have smiled, but her nerves would not allow her as she gingerly sat back in the chair. Harry slowly raised the cape and gave it a good flick. It cracked like a stock whip.

"Let the show begin," he said, as he theatrically flung the cape around Ali's shoulders and fastened it at the back. Harry took a step backwards as Jonathan moved forward.

"I want you to trust me, Ali. Can you do that? I am about to transform you," he said, resting a reassuring hand on her shoulder. Ali hesitated and gripped the arms of the chair, but relaxed and concentrated on her breathing slowly, in–and–out. "Okay, I trust you." Her commitment was weak, but Jonathan took it as gospel.

With a nod from Jonathan, Harry flicked a switch and instantaneously Abba appeared on the screen above the mirror and *Dancing Queen* came blaring out of the surround-sound speakers. Ali rolled her eyes and cursed under her breath.

The men were too involved with how they would style Ali's hair and colour-match her make-up to pay attention to what she was saying. They flittered about the room, in time with the music, holding up hairpieces and colour charts against her skin. Ali sat patiently for hours while the men coloured and preened her hair. The pulling and tugging at her head, as hair extensions were being attached was too much, and so Ali used the technique taught to her by her therapist, Edith Black, and went deeper and deeper into her meditation. The music and the men's voices faded into the background as Edith Black's voice became clearer in her mind. *"How are you feeling tonight, Ali?" Edith asked. "Ok."*

In her mind, Ali was back at the clinic. She could clearly see herself sitting on a white plastic chair facing Edith. Her eyes were closed. *Edith monitored Ali's nervous behaviour, repeatedly rubbing the inside of her arm. Her movements were slow and deliberate, as if trying to wipe away something offensive.*

"Ali."

"Yes."

"I'd like you to open your eyes and look at me."

Ali didn't respond. Edith repeated her request.

"I can't." Ali finally said on the brink of hysteria. "I can't," she said, several times more.

"It's alright, Ali. Keep your eyes closed. Breathe, in – and – out."

When Ali settled, Edith spoke again. "Would you like to tell me why you can't open your eyes?"

Ali sat upright and very still. After a long pause, she began fidgeting again.

"Are you uncomfortable, Ali?" She shook her head, "No" crackled from the back of her throat. "I, I can't look at the veins on my arms. I can't open my eyes."

"Why can't you open your eyes and why can't you look at your veins, Ali?"

"Because when I do, I want a fix – and, and I'll die. I can't die. I have to get better. I have to."

"What runs through your veins, Ali?"

Ali's eyes sprang open, surprised at the question, "What?"

"What runs through your veins?"

Ali thought for a moment, "Blood," she answered, puzzled.

"Right!" Edith smiled. "And what happens when blood runs through your veins?"

After she had given some thought to the question, she said, "Life," but in the same instant she said, "I don't deserve to live: I don't deserve anything ..."

The scene in the session room faded slowly into the background of her mind, as the distant sound of the men's voices calling her name brought her back to consciousness.

"Oh, you've come back," she heard one of them say. They spun the chair around for Ali to review her new look in the mirror. Still groggy, she stared at the strangely familiar image. The men waited, expecting her to be thrilled.

Ali's eyes glistened. She dabbed them with the edge of the cape, then looked back at the reflection she recognised as the child's at the shore's edge playing with her little brother, all grown up and renewed. Ali's shoulder-length ebony curls fell every which way when she moved. A curl fell across her right eye, so she flicked it out of the way.

"Oh my God," Ali mumbled, studying her reflection; her skin was flawless – the tattoos, marks of rebellion, and the ugly scars across her throat and on her arms were invisible. *'I'm clean and new.'*

Jonathan and Harry's rapturous expression dissolved when Ali began to sob.

"What is it, Ali?" Jonathan yelled out over the music, hovering around her, flapping his hands like a swan with a broken wing.

"Yes, yes, what's wrong"? Harry broke in, "Don't you like our work? We used the best quality products, Ali. Your extensions are Russian hair, the best hair money can buy, and the cosmetics are French." He prattled on, trying his best to console her.

Ali was trying to speak, but couldn't. Her sobbing had turned to full throttle. "It's," sniff, sniff, "it's, wonderful! I look," sniff, "a-maz-ing!"

The men released a heavy sigh and grinned at each other. They left Ali to settle down while they cleaned up. A short time later, Jonathan swanned up to Ali and offered, "White tea, black tea, white coffee or a short black?"

Ali gave him a puzzled look. She thought there was something familiar about the way Jonathan said that, like she had heard him say it before. But how could she, when they have just met?

"Coffee, white, thanks," she replied shyly.

Ali looked up at Jonathan when he returned and handed her the cup and saucer and coyly said, "Thank you, Jonathan and you too, Harry." She shook her head puzzled, and shrugged. "I don't know what's happening to me. I'm not a sook. Never was. It's this place."

"What?" Harry queried, "The salon?" giving Ali a sideways glance, as he rifled through the make-up case putting a small make-up and skincare kit together for her.

"No. This village, oh, I don't know. I'm not sure," she shrugged with uncertainty,

"Maybe the café, I don't know. I feel so emotional. I can't explain why. I've been through a lot of crap and I've never cried about it, but now, I just don't get it."

Jonathan went quiet, recalling when he and Harry first arrived. "Ali, perhaps fate, the universe – whatever, has brought you here the same way it did us, ten years ago." Jonathan looked over at Harry and said, "Do you recall when we first arrived?"

Harry nodded. "We both were hard of heart and pessimistic," Jonathan said, turning back to Ali. "We wallowed in wine and drugs, that was eons ago though," he quickly added. "A bus detour also brought us to this village. We changed dramatically within hours of arriving." He turned back to Harry, "Didn't we?" Harry nodded again and added, "You're correct in thinking there's something *special* about the café, Ali. We felt it too."

"Look guys, I'd better explain something. I didn't come from a broken home. My family are amazing. I just got mixed up with the wrong crowd at a promotion party one night. I was modelling for a Melbourne fashion house at the time. I tried recreational drugs and, bam! At sixteen, I was hooked. My life changed in an instant. I was out of control – messed up at school and was expelled. I ended up on the street. It broke my parents' hearts the way I was. They dragged me home and sent me to rehab in Europe – twice. After all the pain I caused them, I want to stay clean. I've got to stay clean or I will end up dead. It's as simple as that."

Harry cleared his throat. "Would you mind if I ask a personal question? You don't have to answer."

Ali ran her fingers over her throat, "This? How did I get this?"

"Yes."

Ali hung her head. Her voice sounded shaky when she spoke, "My boyfriend. He's the son of a well-known celeb. He's crazy! He tried to kill me. He's in prison now, got three years, but he'll be out in a year. He said he'll come after me when does. I know he will. I left Melbourne so my family would be safe. I can't go back and my family must never find out where I am, either. I can't risk my ex hurting them."

"You'll be safe here, Ali. We'll guarantee it," Harry declared. Jonathan stepped forward to show his support also.

"By the way guys," she said with a grin, "The salon's mind–blowing."

Their faces almost split in two, beaming with pride.

"At first it freaked me out. It looked familiar but I couldn't think why. Then I remembered my mum used to go to a salon in Melbourne, just like this one. I was about nine then."

Jonathan caught his breath and grabbed Harry's arm. "What's your mother's name, Ali?"

"Elizabeth Swanson. Why?"

His hand shot up and covered his mouth as he gave Harry a sly glance ignoring the fear in his eyes. "Oh – my -God," Jonathan raved on concealing the contempt he felt towards Elizabeth, "*you* are Alison Swanson! I remember you. "Oh-my-God!" He sang, flapping his hands and squealing with delight. "I did Elizabeth's hair when the boss was away." He stopped and placed his hands on his hips and primly announced, "I was one of the senior stylists at the salon. Top senior, of course. Your mother did commercials, didn't she? I remember the wine commercial ..."

It was midnight by the time the evening came to an end and the men walked Ali back to her cabin. Although there was not a soul in sight, the night was alive. Crickets and geckos singing to their hearts' content had a back-up choir of frogs, and other eerier creatures glowed in the moonlight. When they reached her cabin, Ali thanked the men profusely a second time and then bade them a goodnight. As she disappeared through her doorway, the men grinned at each other with malicious intent and mouthed, "It's pay-back time."

7

In an apartment building overlooking the Yarra River, in the heart of Melbourne, Elizabeth Swanson sat at her computer going through a long list of emails. Her large green eyes carefully perused them all, day after day, searching for the one from her daughter, Alison. Although she told her parents she would not contact them, Elizabeth kept hoping all the same. She could hear her daughter's voice in her mind, pleading with her to understand. *"I can't tell you or Dad, Mum, I don't know where I'm going myself. Even if I did, I still wouldn't tell you. If you don't know, Rhys won't harm either of you…"*

Vivid lighting bouncing off the computer screen lit up Elizabeth's face. The fine lines encompassing her eyes and generous mouth revealed the pain she was feeling, but Elizabeth continued scrolling down the page regardless, hoping. She came across an unfamiliar email and clicked it open and recoiled.

"Steven! Steven!" She called, suppressing the urge to retch, covering her mouth with her hand.

"What is it, love?" her husband hollered from his office next door, "I'm coming," and was at Elizabeth's side in a flash. All that exercise was doing him some good, he was thinking, aware that he was not out of breath from the dash. "What is it, darling?"

Elizabeth sat motionless with her eyes glued to the screen, totally bewildered at the reprehensible, hateful and threatening words. She moved her hand from her mouth and pointed at the screen. Steven muttered parts of the message… *"You fucking bitch!!! I'll get you if it's the last thing I do. I won't stop until you are dead. Liar!! I will destroy you. You lying fucking, cunt, bitch!!!! Kill yourself!!!"*

He turned to his wife, "Who would send this, this, venom?"

Elizabeth did not answer. Her eyes glistened as the reality of the email hit her, *'someone wants to harm me, but why?'*

"Oh Steven, could it be possible that Rhys Ashby sent this from prison? Alison did warn us."

"I've no idea, love, perhaps."

"Oh God," she cried miserably," I wish I knew where Alison is and if she's safe. Where's our daughter, Steven? She's been gone for so many months, without a word from her."

"I'm calling the police!" Steven declared.

"No! You can't. Alison begged us not to. The Ashbys are too influential …"

"Well, she didn't say anything about not hiring a private investigator," he winked.

8

Julia arrived promptly after Olivia's phone call. "Where would you like me to start, Mum?" she asked, surveying the room as if preparing for battle, notebook in one hand and pen in the other.

"You're a lifesaver, love. It's been so hectic – last booth at the end. Watch out though, those yoga gals are a rowdy lot," Olivia winked, "it's Francesca's birthday."

As Julia approached their booth, she overheard some of the conversation.

"He said yeah, Ma, I can see you're wearing your winter skin," and the four women at the table roared with laughter. "So I'm not fat. I'm just wearing my winter skin, all year round," Francesca Cahill was saying.

"Sounds good to me," Julia quipped over the ruckus.

"Hi Jules!" Francesca shrieked, jumping up to hug her. "It's been a while. Helping out today?" Francesca pointed to her friends, "Remember the gals, Jules?"

"Yes, it has been a while. I am helping out today," Julia laughed, "and yes, I sure do remember the gals. How could I not?" She grinned, scanning the attractive faces of Nicky Porter, Maree Morgan and Rose James. "Still going to yoga classes?" she chuckled, "They were a blast."

The women grinned sheepishly at each other and then at Julia.

"Now, Jules," Nicky chipped in, looking coy, "Do we look like we still do yoga? Can't you see we're wearing our winter skins?" She glanced at the others and winked, and they responded with chuckles.

Julia's brow creased, "You're what? Oh yeah, the winter skin," she said, raising her brows knowingly. "Well, I think you all look fabulous."

"Oh come on, Jules, we know that's a polite way of saying we've gained weight," Nicky chirped, kick-starting the hilarity. "It's Olivia's fault we're chubbers," she added.

Julia's eyes narrowed a little, "How so?"

"Her yummy cakes and delicious tucker," Nicky grinned mischievously, "They're just too yummy to resist. Speaking of food, where's that menu? I'm starving."

"Me too," echoed the others in unison.

The women quietened down long enough for Julia to take their orders and to wish Francesca a happy birthday. She walked away chuckling softly to herself, thinking about the evenings they all spent together. Initially, Julia had met them at her Monday night yoga class. She never missed a class, until her marriage to Ben and a busy work schedule absorbed her free time.

'They were unpredictable, but so much fun.' Julia thought, recalling those evenings with fondness. *'None of them could be serious for a moment. They were disruptive, incorrigible and spontaneous.'* A broad smile escaped, as the scenes of all of them together in class ran like a movie in her mind *Maree or Rose would usually whisper a joke or do something outrageous that would send laughter tumbling through the class like a tidal wave. She could even see the frustrated yoga coach clenching her jaw, as the group acted*

more like naughty children than adults. And Nicky's yoga outfit, 'Oh – my - Gawd! That iridescent pink and lime green Lycra thing, with a matching headband and legwarmers was hideous.' Julia shook her head in amusement as she visualised her friend in the get-up. The scene came alive in her thoughts as she carried on working.

Julia recalled the conversation between Nicky, affectionately known as Nic, and Maree the first time Nic wore her new outfit to the class.

"We're not getting physical, Nic," Maree playfully teased her for wearing the eighties reject. "We're doing yoga." Maree gave Nicky the once over and screwed up her face in disgust. "I didn't know you could still buy that stuff. It was awful back in the eighties and it's even worse now."

"I know, I know," Nic whined, shrugging her left shoulder the way a small child would. "I don't feel good in tracky daks. I need to feel firm. Lycra holds in my tummy."

"But why that colour?"

"I look pretty in pink."

"Pretty? Really?"

"Yes!"

"Ah! C'mon," Maree sighed in mild frustration, tugging on her friend's sleeve, "We'd better go before the class starts."

Madison looked up when Julia came into the kitchen laughing. "What's so funny?"

"Oh, nothing really. I just remembered how much I enjoyed my yoga classes."

"Do you go to yoga classes?" Madison asked.

"Not anymore."

When the last of the customers left, Olivia put the *'Closed'* sign on the door. She made three coffees and then flopped down on one of the stools at the counter.

"I'll put something together for us after I catch my breath. But right now, all I want is this coffee. Come on you two, join me."

Julia and Madison were bushed too, and did not hesitate in dropping what they were doing to sit down.

"Is it like this every Sunday, Mum?"

Madison nodded before Olivia could answer.

"You've got to hire more staff, Mum. An extra hand in the kitchen would be wonderful, and one more out front wouldn't hurt either."

"I know, I know," Olivia agreed, rubbing her forehead. She was so drained that she could hardly think straight.

"I'm going to ask Francesca. She mentioned the other day that she was looking for full-time work. She's methodical, and a great cook." Olivia paused a moment and then said hesitantly, "There's something else I have to tell you."

Madison and Julia nodded their approval of Francesca. But the ominous sound in Olivia's voice put them on alert. Olivia almost choked on her coffee when she saw concern in their eyes.

"Oh, no," she laughed, "it's nothing that serious. Well, I hope not anyway."

"Well, what is it then?" Julia queried.

Olivia hesitated, then blurted out, "I hired a girl this morning and, and well – she's different."

"Different? How?" Julia frowned.

"I'm not sure how to explain, Ali Swanson. That's her name. She's different, that's all. You can see for yourselves in the morning."

Everyone went silent and then suddenly Julia shrugged and jumped up.

"Okay, but right now, I'm famished. I'll go and put something together for us."

Madison gathered up the cups and followed her, "I'll help you."

"You're amazing, sweetheart."

Olivia turned her gaze from the window to the stool beside her. Anton was sitting there smiling at her. "I couldn't be amazing without you," she whispered to him.

"I'll be here for you, for as long as you need me."

Julia and Madison returned with a large plate, full of sandwiches. They both sat down with a heavy sigh.

"You were supposed to be my guest today, love." Olivia apologised to Julia.

"Anytime, Mum. I've had so much fun and even caught up with Francesca and the girls. They're still daft as ever," she laughed, "in a good way, of course."

"What time is Ben's flight due?" Olivia asked looking up at the clock.

Julia glanced down at her watch. "Oh heck, I'd better hurry. I've got an hour to get home, shower, change and get to the airport before his connecting flight arrives up here. I'm sorry we don't have more time, Mum." Julia was saying as she was gathering her things together and hugging Olivia goodbye.

"We'll see you tomorrow though. Ben's taking a few days off. His work schedule has been manic. The practice is booming. He employed another solicitor last week. That's three now. My darling needs a break. And you haven't seen your son in ages."

Olivia was smiling, "I'll see you both in the morning. Now get going and drive carefully. Bye, love."

"Bye Mum, bye Madison."

"Bye, Jules."

9

Julia left with a heavy heart. Her mind was in overdrive as she drove to Segal Bay's light aircraft airport. Although Julia enjoyed her day with Olivia, she had hoped to prepare her for Ben's overseas job offer.

'Ah well,' Julia shrugged, *'can't be helped. Ben and I will tell her together, tomorrow.'*

Julia turned into the airport car park just in time to see Ben heading for the far end of the footpath, where he usually waited for her.

'It's amazing how much he resembles his father's photograph,' she mused, *'he hasn't a clue how handsome he is. He turns heads wherever he goes. Aaaaah! my beautiful unassuming man, just look at that smile.'*

"Hi, Honey! How was the trip?" Julia beamed when Ben opened the car door.

"Great, baby!" He chirped, tossing his bag in the back and jumping in beside her, "It would've been even better if you'd have been with me. I miss you when you're not with me," he said, pouting.

"Good answer," she laughed, "You get special attention when we get home."

"Mmmmm! Sounds good to me. We can start now," and he began caressing her neck.

She kissed him and playfully slapped his arm, telling him to behave.

"Guess where I was today?"

"I give in, where?"

"At the café. I had a ball working there today, but I'm not making a career change, that's for sure. I like working for my gorgeous husband," she laughed and went on, "The café's *booming*. I don't know how Mum does it. The place was packed for most of the day. Francesca starts tomorrow, and there's someone else as well. Mum sounded concerned about the new girl. I'm not sure why though, she wouldn't say."

"Did you manage to tell Mum about our plans?" Ben asked when Julia took a breath.

"No, we were too busy, but on second thought, I think we should tell her together."

"Yeah, I suppose you're right. I'm really dreading the idea of telling her we're moving to the opposite side of the globe." Ben looked seriously at Julia, "You know, Jules, I feel guilty about going, for wanting to go. I feel I'm deserting her. I'm really torn."

Julia gently rested her hand on Ben's knee. "I'm sorry, sweetheart that I don't have a magic wand to fix everything. I wish I had the answer, but I don't. It's your call, baby. I'll support you, whatever you choose to do."

Ben slipped their favourite CD into the player and leaned back in his seat as *'The Boss'* lifted their mood with his words and music. It was their song, their pledge to each other:

"We said we'd walk together baby come what may.

That come the twilight should we lose our way.

If as we're walkin' a hand should slip free, I'll wait for you and should I fall behind wait for me ..."

As the music filled the vehicle, Ben nonchalantly reached up and ran his hand through Julia's hair, as he hummed along with Bruce. A peace crept over him. She did that to him. He turned and looked at her and smiled. Headlights of passing cars propelled shapeless shadows across her lovely face and lit up the red strands in her hair; her eyes momentarily sparkled like emeralds when the headlights hit them.

'This beautiful woman is my wife,' Ben was thinking, and sighed lightly, *'I'm a lucky man.'*

Julia turned when Ben sighed, "Tired?"

"Mmmm, more relaxed than tired, I'd say. I'm just glad to be home, home with you!"

"Aaaaah, you're such a suck," Julia teased, "that's why I love you."

"Do you?" Ben exclaimed in mocked surprise.

She playfully slapped him again, "You're gunna get it when we get home."

"Ooh! I can hardly wait." He laughed, and then fell silent and listened to their song:

... we swore we'd travel, Darlin' side by side
We'd help each other stay in stride.
But each lovers step falls so differently.
But I'll wait for you and if I should I fall behind wait for me.
Now everyone dreams of a love last and true.
But you and I know what this world can do.
So let's make our step clear that the other may see.
And if I should fall behind wait for me. Now there's a beautiful river in the valley ahead.
There 'neath the oak bough soon we will be wed.

Should we lose each other in the shadow of the evening trees.
I'll wait for you and should I fall behind wait for me. Darlin' I'll wait for you, should I fall behind wait for me."

Julia turned off the main road as the song finished and they drove the rest of the way home in contented silence.

The car lights flashing on the bedroom wall announced Ben and Julia's arrival. O'Malley stirred and stretched out as far as he could, and then rolled on his back and waited for them to come and fuss over him.

"O'Malley, you brazen fur ball!" Julia laughed when she found their moggie stretched out on their bed, "You're a vulgar boy, showing all your boy bits like that," she said, lovingly, scratching his belly. When she stopped, the old boy got up and bolted to the end of the bed meowing in protest for more attention.

"Ok, just a little more, but I've got things to do – like get your dinner."

He was purring loudly and then stopped. He sat up and meowed and then leaped off the bed like a shot out of a gun and ran to the kitchen, stopping in front of his dish and patiently waited.

"What are we going to do with the big fella when we leave? We can't take him with us?"

O'Malley looked up, watching and listening to them talking. He meowed and they both looked down at him.

"You know, Jules, if I didn't know better, I'd swear he understands what we're saying."

She nodded. "I sometimes get that feeling too - I know where he can go."

"Mum's!" They both said, "She adores him."

Julia smiled and crouched down beside O'Malley and scratched his chin.

10

At the end of the day, Olivia locked up and headed home. She enjoyed walking the short distance, it gave her time to unwind and go over the day in her mind.

Late summer afternoons were always glorious. A warm, gentle breeze ruffled her hair and clothing and the sky was awash with stunning colours. Olivia stopped a moment to admire nature at its best, full of gratitude for the sheer pleasure of witnessing a splendid sight. She was thinking how much she enjoyed working with Julia and was looking forward to seeing her and Ben in the morning. Olivia smiled as she thought about how thrilled and grateful Francesca was to be offered the job. 'Ha! If she only knew how much I need her. I'm run off my feet.'

"Ben's got something important to tell you, darling," Anton said, interrupting Olivia's reflective mood. "I want you to be prepared."

"Is it serious? Is he or Julia ill?" Olivia asked, concerned. "Oh dear, what is it?"

"No, no, it's not serious. Ben's been offered a consultant position with an Italian firm in Rome."

His words hit her like a heavy-handed slap. The colour drained from her face.

"But, but," Olivia stammered in an effort to speak, but the words would not come.

"Ben wants to take it, darling, but he's worried about you," Anton continued. "He feels guilty for wanting to go. Darling, he feels he's deserting you."

When Olivia arrived at her front door, she stood perplexed, holding the keys in her hand trying to imagine life in Segal Bay without her son and Julia. She could only feel a profound pain in her heart. "No!" she said out loud, "I'm not having any of this," and shook off the dreaded feeling that was trying to corral her.

Later that evening, Olivia put on her favourite classical CD. It played softly in the background as she relaxed; submerged to her chin in the *ofuro*, Anton built after they returned from a Japanese tour. They both embraced the Japanese custom of bathing; with the shedding of their clothes, so goes their daily concerns. One lathers up and rinses off thoroughly before climbing into the deep *ofuro* of hot water: a time for relaxing, a time for well-being, and a time for washing away the troubles of the day. When Anton built the *ofuro*, he added two extra water tanks to the side of the house, so they could use the tub as often as they liked. Olivia was usually too busy to indulge herself.

'There are times,' she was thinking, *'when one just has to surrender to a pampering. Tonight's one of those times.'*

"Cheers, darling," she smiled, lifting her wine glass up to Anton, who was standing by the door. "Now what's this about Ben going overseas?"

"I don't want you worrying about that, dear heart, just let things fall where they may. Ben and Julia have their paths to follow, just as you have."

"What does that mean?"

"I can't tell you, but I promise to be here with you, for as long as you need me."

Olivia had anticipated Ali's first day would be challenging and worried how she would fit in working at the café. *'Ah well, I guess it's too late to worry about that now,'* she thought, *'here goes nothing,'* and drew in a long breath and put the key in the café door.

"Good morning, Olivia. Hope you don't mind that I'm early."

Olivia momentarily froze, and then slowly turned around, clasping hold of her jacket as if it were some sort of support, dreading what she was about to face.

"Good morn…Oh my God!" Olivia cried. Her eyes almost popped from their sockets, "You're beautiful, Ali. The boys have certainly worked their magic on you; there's *no* trace of *that* girl who walked into my café yesterday morning."

Olivia was so relieved that she lunged forward and hugged her without thinking

Ali grinned coyly. "Yeah, well – you can imagine my reaction to the new me. It's been a long time since I've seen this uncool Ali – but I like her," she quickly added, with a lopsided grin.

Olivia laughed a deep joyful laugh. "Is the new Ali ready to work as a kitchen hand and waitress?"

"This new girl is so ready!"

"Well then, let's get started," Olivia said, handing Ali a work schedule as soon as they entered the kitchen. "You can't go wrong if you follow these instructions – it's that simple, Ali but ask if you need help or are unsure of anything, ok?"

Ali was going over the instructions when Francesca arrived. Since Francesca had often filled in as cook on busy days, she knew what she had to do and set to work after the introductions.

Later that morning, when Jonathan and Harry came in for breakfast, Olivia dashed out to the dining room and congratulated them on Ali's transformation.

Ali also saw them come in and followed Olivia. Francesca was curious as to what had made both of them rush to the dining room. She craned her neck just far enough to see who it was, *'Ah huh, those two.'*

The mixer, screaming like a bush banshee beating butter, vanilla and powdered sugar into a fluffy cream, drowned out their conversation, but by the men's animated gestures and hugs from Olivia and Ali, Francesca knew they were gloating about something. Olivia turned around suddenly and caught a glimpse of Francesca's expression. Although Olivia thought it was odd, she did not say anything to Francesca when she returned to the kitchen.

By mid-morning the breakfast rush was down to a crawl. Olivia was elated. Everything had run smoothly. She was thanking Ali and Francisca when Ben and Julia waltzed into the kitchen.

"Hi, Mum!" they said in unison, doing their best to sound cheerful, "What's for breakfast?"

They waved to Francisca. She smiled and carried on icing a tray of cupcakes.

Ali stopped scrubbing the pan she was holding and looked over her shoulder. *'My God,'* she thought, *'he's gorgeous. Where have I seen him before? She's beautiful too.'*

Olivia placed the knife she was using on the bench, wiped her hands on her apron and spread her arms open wide as she walked towards them.

"My darlings! Whatever you want," she said, wrapping her arms around Ben who towered over her and hugged him tight. She released him and moved over to Julia and hugged her.

"Ali!" Olivia called, "Come over here and say hello to my son, Ben, and my daughter-in-law, Julia."

Julia studied the tall, attractive, fresh-faced girl with the shiny raven hair pulled back into a ponytail, standing by the sink, looking for signs of what was different about her, but could not see anything unusual. Julia nonchalantly shrugged and thought, *'Ali looks normal to me. Hmm, I'm not sure what Mum meant by her being different, except that she's very beautiful and those lavender eyes are amazing!'*

Ali smiled and said, "Hello." Ben offered her his hand. Although the contact between them was brief, she felt a tingle in her hand. Julia saw Ali's reaction to Ben and smiled. She was used to women succumbing to his charm and was not bothered by it. It was what she loved about him.

"Lovely to meet you, Ali," Julia smiled when they shook hands, "You arrived in the nick of time. Mum really needs help."

"And a great help she is too. So is Francesca. Everything ran like clockwork this morning. Anyway, since we're on schedule, I'll join you for a coffee and we can catch up on all your news. Your favourite table is vacant, so go over and sit down and I'll join you in a minute."

Olivia turned her face sideways and grinned when Ben and Julia's smiles vanished at the mentioning of, '...catch up on your news'. *'Let them squirm a little,'* she thought with amusement.

They were whispering to each other when Olivia arrived with the food; she would have been concerned had she not known their secret. Olivia knew her jovial mood was making it difficult for them to tell her of their plans. She hummed along with the tune playing on the jukebox and her large brown eyes sparked as she lovingly smiled at Ben and Julia when she put their breakfast in front of them. She then gently stroked their hair and said in sing-song, "Eat up, darlings." Neither Ben nor Julia touched their food. They sat, slump-shouldered and forlorn, staring at their plates.

"What's wrong, my darlings?" Olivia cooed, enjoying their discomfort "That's your favourite breakfast. My goodness, you two," she playfully teased, folding her arms in mock concern, "If I didn't know better, I'd say you've something ominous to tell me like, running away to the other side of the world or something."

They both squirmed in their seat, as if sitting on nails. Ben sucked in air and with a surge of courage said, "Well Mum, since you've mentioned running away, er, I mean..." He cleared his throat and blurted out. "There is no way to soften this, so I'll just say it: I've been offered a job overseas and I really want to take it. It's a fantastic opportunity and…"

"That's wonderful, darling," Olivia broke in, "When do you have to leave? O'Malley, of course, will stay with me."

Their jaws fell open and their eyes grew as large as dinner plates in disbelief; they had worried themselves sick over a non-event.

11

Olivia was overjoyed with the way her business was flourishing, owing the success of the café to the harmony within its walls, "And, of course, to my wonderful staff," she would say, when passing tourists commented of the café's popularity.

Ali was like a breath of fresh air for the café. The locals and tourists embraced her and her quirky ways with open arms; and the residents from Manor Retirement Village across the street adored her.

Tom Fisher was one of the newer residents there. When he adamantly rebuffed invitations from some of the women at Manor Village to join them for card games and outings, word quickly circulated that he was abrasive and woebegone: Tom's daughter, Anne Jackson, had hoped a sea-change would soothe her father's temperament; to the contrary, Tom became more withdrawn and belligerent. In desperation to get him out of his apartment and mingle with other people, Anne insisted that they go to the café across the street and have lunch, before she went home to her husband and two sons.

Anne studied her lean, elderly father who sat opposite and felt sad. He looked like a cardboard cut-out, sitting erect and very still, staring out of the café window. Filtered light coming in from the street fell on Tom's tired and transparent skin, highlighting the tiny veins that ran in every direction under the delicate hide. His pale blue eyes seemed lifeless. Having recently lost his beloved wife of sixty years, and combating constant pain which racked his weary limbs, and with every bone in his body on fire, the essence of joy had dissolved from within his soul.

Something Tom saw out of the corner of his eye made him turn away from the window, and look at what was going on around him. Anne noticed her father stretch his worn frame into a more comfortable position. In disbelief she witnessed the creased, delicate skin around his mouth stretch wide and smooth across his aged, stained teeth and his sad eyes dance back to life when a tall, slender girl with a ponytail swaying from side to side like a pendulum, sashayed up to their booth.

"Hey, Dude, how ya doin'!" Ali beamed, handing menus to Tom and his startled daughter.

****

Six months on, Ali still had that same effect on Tom. "Has the kitchen at the Village run out of tucker?" Ali teased, while taking Tom's breakfast order.

Tom laughed softly, "No, love, I've just come in for my injection of sunshine. That's about all I can do at my age, and some days even that's a challenge," he smiled warmly, and thought Ali's smile reminded him of Ruth.

"Now don't go selling yourself short, Tom." Ali said seriously, "You're a cool dude. You should hook up with one of those chicks from the Village," inclining her head towards the four women sitting at the far end of the room playing mah-jong, "and hit the town sometime."

Tom's deep belly laugh was loud enough for the patrons sitting nearby to look his way. "Even thinking about what you're suggesting, Ali, would be the end of me. And by the way, love, there are no chicks in my backyard, we're all old boilers."

"Well, you know what they say, Dude, where there's life, there's always hope," she winked. "What are you having today?"

"French toast and coffee, thanks, love. Let's hope I can manage to get through breakfast without mishap," he kidded.

"We have bibs for dribblers," she laughed, running off to the kitchen.

In no time, Tom was relaxing back in the booth, leisurely eating his breakfast while observing his surroundings with profound gratitude. He chewed his food slowly, savouring the flavours of the banana, maple syrup and pan fried bread, dipped in egg and milk. Tom smiled with satisfaction each time he swallowed. Ali had recommended this gastronomic delight the first week he came to the café.

'Everyone seems relaxed and happy here,' he considered with pleasure. The four women from the village Ali mentioned were still playing Mahjong and, by their expressions, the game was serious. A sudden burst of laughter and cheers announced that the game was over.

Maggie Andrews looked up from counting her Mahjong tiles, getting ready for another game, and smiled when she noticed Tom looking their way. Her smile brightened when Tom waved. He watched the women with interest as they jovially chatted among themselves. Maggie was humming the *Tennessee Waltz* tune coming from the jukebox as she played and then all four women burst into song. The room thundered with applause when the song ended.

'This place has marvellous atmosphere', Tom thought, feeling indebted to Anne for insisting they come here for lunch

six months ago. *'If she hadn't been so insistent, I would have missed out on all this and meeting Ali.'*

Tom sat tall and smiled broadly, *'Ali is not afraid of me. Only Ruth and Ali saw through my armour.'* The smile quickly turned to a thoughtful crease in Tom's brow. *'Men of my generation don't show their feelings like men do these days. We worked and we worked hard with no nonsense about it.'* He nodded to himself to make a point. *'Men provided for their families. It was our duty and that was that.'*

Tom's features softened when he thought about his wife. *'Ruth was a wonderful and loving woman. She was my best friend,'* he continued, *'and Anne, well she is a good daughter, but I wish she wasn't so timid around me. I've never punished her, ah well. A man should just count his blessings I suppose,'* Tom sighed. *'Anne is a good girl and she's doing her best with her cranky old dad.'* He smiled and carried on reflecting. *'We do have wonderful conversations these days, I must at least be grateful for that.'*

Tom got up precariously from the table when he had finished his meal, and dropped a $10.00 note on the side plate for Ali. He waved to her on his way out. She watched him through the window walk slowly to the kerb. *'Tom's a really cool guy.'* Ali had no way of knowing how grateful Tom was to her for bringing him back to life, never dreaming that he would ever laugh again after his beloved Ruth died. But he did, thanks to Ali. Tom turned around and waved again, just before he stepped from the kerb. Ali was waving back when she suddenly shrilled, "Tom, watch out!" sending shockwaves through the café. He had not seen the lights change. The impact shot Tom's body into the air, over the vehicle and onto the pavement, landing with a heavy thud.

People bolted from the café and congregated in the street with passing tourists and surfers, "Call triple O," someone shouted.

Ali was hysterical and was about to run outside too, but Olivia grabbed her by the arm and gently pulled her back. "It's my fault! It's my fault!" She shrieked. "Tom was looking at me. He didn't see the car. Let me go, Olivia."

"You don't need to see him, sweetheart. There's nothing you can do for Tom. Olivia said softly, gently rocking Ali as she looked up at Anton. He was shaking his head, confirming Tom had gone. "I think Tom's with Ruth now." Olivia said, hoping to soothe her.

Through her tears Ali asked, "Who's Ruth?"

"Tom's wife, she passed away about a year ago. Her death shattered him."

"Oh! So that's why he seemed so sad when he first came in here?" Ali remarked. "So you reckon Tom's ok and is with his wife?"

"I do. I certainly do. Anton's with me, so why wouldn't Tom be with Ruth?"

Ali looked puzzled when Olivia mentioned Anton being with her, but was too upset to ask what she had meant by that.

"I'll miss him, Olivia," Ali moaned. "Tom's a nice man. I mean, was a nice man."

12

A few days after Tom's funeral, Anne Jackson came in to the Corner Café. Francesca was behind the counter, filling coffee orders. When Francesca saw Anne, she signalled to Madison. "Finish these orders, love, while I fetch Ali."

"Ali!" Francesca whispered, rushing to the storeroom. "Where are you?"

"Up here, top of the ladder. What's up?" Ali whispered back. "Why are we whispering?"

"Come down right away! Tom's daughter's in the dining room. I imagine she's looking for you."

"Bet she blames me for Tom's death. Now I'm in for it." Ali grumbled, stepping down from the ladder.

"Tom's death was an accident, kiddo. No one blames you. Just go and find out what she wants."

"Ok Francesca, I will, but you'd better stay close by, just in case she tries to do me in."

Before Ali faced Anne, she took several deep breaths, remembering Edith's instruction to breathe to remain calm. When composed, and with a surge of false confidence, Ali entered the dining room.

Anne saw Ali and scrambled out of the booth. "Ali! How are you?"

"Hi Anne, er, I'm fine, thanks. How about you? I'm so sorry about your dad?"

"Thank you, Ali. Can we talk? I wanted to catch up with you at the funeral, but you had left."

"About what?"

"Dad, he asked me to come. Please, it's important."

Ali stuttered, "He, he, did? Why?"

"To thank you."

"Me? For what?"

"Come and sit down…" Ali obeyed and sat opposite Anne, totally mystified.

"Dad and I hardly had a conversation until he met you."

"Why?"

"I didn't really know him growing up. As a child, I went to school and he went to work. That's the way it was in those days. I rarely saw my father and the times I did, he was busy fixing something around the house. Although he was a serious man, Dad was a good man. I wanted for nothing except for his time and his attention. When Mum passed away, Dad just gave up. I couldn't reach him, not until the day I dragged him over here. He got a kick out of you calling him *Dude*. We laughed together about that: we hadn't ever done that before, laughed together, I mean. You were our common interest. At first, all he talked about was you. I must admit I was a little jealous at first but then I realised my father and I were actually having a conversation and that was what I had wanted all my life. He soon began to share stories about Mum and about himself when they were young. It was all because of you, Ali that I finally got to know my father."

Anne took a minute to allow Ali to digest what she saying. Ali remained silent and only moved to brush away rebel tears.

"Dad asked me to give these to you, Ali" Anne said, handing her an envelope and a small, worn, brown leather box. Ali opened the box slowly and discovered it contained an antique gold pocket watch attached to a thick gold chain.

"The watch belonged to Dad," Anne announced proudly. "He treasured it. His father gave it to him the day he graduated from university. Read the inscription. *"Congratulations Son, I believe you will go far in life"*.

Ali was speechless.

"Dad believed in you, Ali, and he expects you to go far in life too. He said you probably played dumb at school because being top of the class was uncool."

Ali knowingly smiled and nodded.

"Now open the envelope," Anne instructed. Ali obeyed and pulled out a cheque for the sum of twenty thousand dollars.

Ali sprang to life. "What the f..." but stopped, "I can't take this Anne," Ali shouted.

"Oh yes you can, and you will. Dad wanted you to have them. You can't refuse his gifts."

"But they're yours, they belong to you."

Anne laid a gentle hand on Ali's arm as she lowered her voice and said,

"Ali, Dad knew he was dying. He had cancer. It was only a matter of weeks. I helped him put his affairs in order. This is what he wanted me to do for him. My father trusted me enough to execute his last request, and I am sure as hell going to do it for him, Ali and you are going to accept this money and the watch. You hear?" she said with conviction.

"Hey there, Anne, ok," Ali replied, holding up both hands. "I give in. If you put it like that, then I accept them. Thank you." Ali sniffed and wiped her eyes. They looked at each other and began laughing, a nervous laugh at first, which quickly turned to jubilation. Anne reached across the table and hugged Ali, saying, "I want you to consider yourself to be a part of my family; Dad would have liked that."

"Well, whatever is going on over here, it sure looks like a celebration that deserves coffee and cake." Francesca declared and added, smiling warmly at Ali and Anne as she put the treats down in front of them. "Our chocolate mud-cake is calorie-free and that's the truth. Enjoy," she said, and walked away humming.

13

Later that afternoon, in her cottage, Ali was sitting at her kitchen table, drinking coffee, trying to rationalise Tom's gifts. *'Today was freaking mind-blowing,'* she thought, churning over in her mind all the things that had happened since she arrived at the Bay.

'Segal Bay is awesome; this place has some sort of magic going on here. I don't understand how I've attracted so much great karma and my addiction has vanished, no hanging out for a fix, it's freaking amazing,' she sighed heavily with relief, *'yep, freaking amazing. Don't smoke anymore either. Not that I'm whinging about it, I'm just freaking amazed. It's so awesome! And now this, I guess Tom expects me to do the chef's course I told him I was saving for. Wow!* she thought, *shaking her head, seriously surprised.*

While the cheque and watch lay idle on the table, Ali held the small, leather box in her hands, periodically turning it over, flipping it open and shut, trying to digest the generosity shown to her. Still holding the box, Ali gently pushed her chair away from the table, got up, grabbed her coffee and strolled out onto the veranda. She closed her eyes and drew in the evening air and slowly released it, grateful to be alive; a pleasant cocktail of rainforest, sea and frangipani scent lingered in the warm air. Her eyes opened and she looked out at the heavens; a few remnants of deep-purple, gold and cyclamen ribbons were still visible as night blanketed the remains of twilight. Birds fell silent as insects and frogs took centre stage; the world around her was at peace.

As time passed, Ali came to a conclusion. "Well then," she said, breaking the silence, "if Tom thought I deserve the money and his treasured watch, then, it's with great honour that I accept them," and raised her coffee mug to salute him.

As another thought came to mind, Ali dashed off to the bedroom and retrieved a folder full of leaflets and a booklet about the chef course she enquired about some weeks ago. She sat at the table and began sorting through the information; she also opened a notebook and began making a to-do list. In the middle of writing, Ali stopped; the excitement bubbling within her suddenly went flat when the image of her parents zoomed into her mind. Guilt tried to consume her, but Ali shook it off quickly, refusing to let sentiment be the catalyst that harms them.

"What I must do right away," said Ali out loud, "is pay Jonathan and Harry for the make-over they gave me, I hate feeling indebted to them." Their repeated refusal of payment she offered for the up-keep of the extensions also concerned her. *'When it's all said and done,'* she reasoned, *'I'm a stranger to them and there's no reason why they should be so overly generous.'* Jonathan's arrogance and his constant reference to her, as his *million dollar* make-over, when they came to the café, bothered her as well. Ali detected a twinge of malice in his tone that she did not understand.

During the morning lull, Ali asked Olivia if she had a minute to talk. Olivia was expecting Ali to say that she was moving on now that she was financially secure. Olivia's eyes enlarged with surprise and absolutely delight when Ali confided in her that she was looking into a chef's course and wanted her advice.

"I really want to do the course, but I don't want to have to leave the Bay," Ali said, looking directly at Olivia who wore an expression that she could not read.

"Hmmm?" was Olivia's response, as a smile slowly creased her attractive features. "I have an idea, but I'll have to make a few enquires first. Ok?"

Ali nodded and said, "I have to bank Tom's cheque and get out cash so I can clear my debt with Jonathan and Harry. My savings will cover it, so would you mind, Olivia, if I take a longer break to get things sorted?"

"Take all the time you need, love."

When Jonathan and Harry came in for lunch, Ali rushed to their table. Wearing a huge smile she handed Jonathan a thick envelope. The men glanced at each other, puzzled.

"What's this?" Jonathan queried.

"Look inside," Ali instructed warmly. Harry leaned in closer as Jonathan lifted the fold of the envelope. "What the…" he gasped in horror when he saw the money. Harry paled. "What's this for?" Jonathan demanded, as his eyes suddenly turned cold and hard.

Ali shuddered and took a step backwards. She had not anticipated this reaction. "It's the money I owe for the make-over," she stammered, "I can afford to pay you now."

"So this is how you appreciate our gesture of kindness? We didn't want any payment. We were doing you a good turn!"

Ali arched up and said that she had always intended to repay them. "Keep the money," she insisted, "it belongs to you and now we're square."

Ali cleared her throat and asked, "Are you gentleman ready to order."

Jonathan glared at her a moment before snatching the envelope from the table and storming out of the café, with Harry rushing to catch up. Ali stood at the table stunned, *'What just happened?'*

As she headed back to the kitchen, Francesca, who saw the whole scene play out from the front counter, cautioned Ali to be careful of the *hairdressers*. "They're both nasty pieces of work."

Ali's eyes widened in disbelief, "They've been so kind to me well, except for just now. I don't get it. Why did Jonathan act like that? He was something else, real scary."

"I wouldn't be surprised if that little creep has a split-personality: dripping sugary sweet compliments like a leaky tap one minute, and the next minute, spitting bullets. His charm never fooled me," Francesca said in an acid tone. "I saw those two for who and what they are the moment I set eyes on them."

Ali was silent, half listening to Francesca, puzzled that she had no clue Jonathan and Harry could be so spiteful. *'They both had been so sweet. What a personality change.'* Then as an afterthought, Ali mentioned that she would have to find a stylist to maintain her hair.

"Oh, I can help you out there," Madison called out from the kitchen, "my mum's the best stylist in town, she's even better than those two narcissists," she winked, coming into the dining room carrying a tray of crockery.

Ali looked over at Francesca for confirmation and Francesca gave her the nod, "I wouldn't let anyone, other than Lilly, touch my hair. She is fantastic and really sweet, on the angelic side, I'd say," Francesca smiled with a twinkle in her eye.

"Give Mum a call and make an appointment," Madison smiled coyly, "Mum knows who you are Ali, that we work together, I mean."

"Ok, thanks Maddie," Ali said, and wrote down the number on a napkin.

14

Jonathan charged down the street as if his pants were on fire. Harry trailed a few steps behind, calling for him to slow down. The scene made foot traffic stop and curiously stare at the pair. The short distance to the salon seemed endless for Harry, cringing with humiliation, while Jonathan relished the theatre and expected Harry to run after him; he would suffer the consequences if he had not.

When they reached the salon, Jonathan let loose: screaming and shouting and calling Ali unimaginable names. "That, that ungrateful junkie, whore, I will get her for doing that!" He shrieked in a feminine high-pitch and threw magazines everywhere. "I hate her! How dare that piece of scum throw my good will in my face! I want her to owe me, not pay me."

Harry was terrified of Jonathan when he flew into his rages. He knew if he said or did anything to antagonise Jonathan, he would get a beating. He remained silent, hoping Jonathan would soon calm down. *'I'll cop it if he can't punish her and it will be her fault. Jonathan never apportions blame.'* Harry thought, as a surge of resentment toward Ali surfaced. *'Why couldn't she just be grateful to us and leave it at that? Why the hell did Ali have to come here in the first place? Jonathan instantly reverted back to his old ways the moment she mentioned her mother's name, ruining our lives.*

While Jonathan was in the back room, Harry meekly went about tidying up after the tornado had passed. As he gathered the magazines off the floor, a glossy, full colour spread of the Ashby Family caught his attention; sparkling eyes and perfect skin and perfect teeth of Madeline, Geoff and their rebel son, Rhys Ashby filled the pages. The celebrity family were announcing the release of their son from prison. *'Rhys is a changed young man,'* said Madeline Ashby of her son. *'He has found God.'* Harry smirked and muttered, "Yeah, I bet he has," and called out to Jonathan who was making coffee.

"What?" he snapped, thumping the bench.

"Look at this," Harry said, rushing to the kitchen and shoving the magazine under Jonathan's nose before he could explode again. As Jonathan read the article, his stern, cold features and pursed lips softened. He glanced up at Harry with evil in his eyes, and then went back to the article. He smiled broadly and cheered, "gotcha!"

Jonathan sat at his computer, gleefully composing an email to Rhys Ashby, telling him he knew of Ali Swanson's whereabouts. The only contact details he had for him was through *Kent & Max*, the law firm mentioned in the article.

Daniel J. Kent was a large man in his sixties, a man of energy and quick wit. His size alone was intimidating enough to command respect. His father, a hard and cruel man, was a womaniser who constantly barked orders at his meek mother and him as a child. Daniel vowed to never simulate his father in any way at all. For a man of his age and stature, Daniel, surprisingly, spoke in soft tones and moved in slow graceful strides. His ethics were strong and honourable. He adored his wife of forty years, two sons and his three grandchildren enough to fire a staff member who constantly flirted with him while they worked in the privacy of his office. One day it became all too much for him to ignore, so he simply told her that she need not bother to come back to the firm, that she was fired. The young woman was shocked and asked what she had done to deserve such a harsh penalty.

"You are an ignorant woman," Daniel calmly said, "who has tried, on numerous occasions, to persuade me to jeopardise my life, my wife, my family and my career. I find you despicable and arrogant that you would even think I would contemplate dishonouring the woman I love. I am a man of my word. I respect and cherish the vows I made to my wife the day we were married."

The morning Jonathan's email arrived, Daniel was at his desk perusing the numerous emails when his shrewd, dark brown eyes spied the ominous email marked *Attention Rhys Ashby*. He read the words with disdain, instinctively knowing the author had an agenda. He shook his head thinking how, at times, he hated his job, protecting insects such as Ashby and others like him. But that was his job to do just that. He worked long and hard hours all his life and became hard-headed and thick-skinned and overcame many obstacles to get to the top of the mountain. Daniel liked where he was and he liked and enjoyed the benefits of being so high on the heap; swimming in the mire was worth it; having the power was worth it. However, there were times he was tempted to leak information to the right people about some of his clients in the name of justice. But Daniel had too much integrity to do that, as he greatly valued his reputation. He reasoned without any contrition, just wanting to sell out the insects, and not doing so meant that he still had a moral code.

His clients paid a small fortune for his services. It was not about whether they were guilty or innocent. For Daniel J Kent it was about the challenge of winning the case. However, the Ashby case was exasperating. His opinion of the Ashby family was low and thought their son abhorrent. He considered Rhys insane and should be incarcerated for the duration of his life. Ashby was unpredictable and dangerous, especially dangerous to Alison Swanson. Daniel was determined not to directly or indirectly assist Ashby in finding her because he knew he would kill her when he did. Daniel J. Kent deleted Jonathan's email.

15

While they were working, Olivia noticed Francesca seemed withdrawn.

"Are you ok, love? She asked concerned, "You haven't been yourself all day."

"You know, Olivia, I've been thinking," Francesca sighed heavily. "Tom's sudden death has highlighted the fact that life is so unpredictable." She stopped wiping down the bench and looked over at Olivia and said, "It's been nearly a year since Julia and Ben left for Italy."

"Yes, I know and thank heavens for the internet. I never dreamt that I would ever use a computer, let alone *surf* the internet and write emails." Olivia laughed. "They feel so much closer since Ben arranged that webcam, we're able to speak face to face when he calls. It's fantastic. It's as if they're next door. It's wonderful".

"I wonder if I will ever travel" Francesca said, "and see the world. Oh! How exciting that would be." There was urgency in Francesca's voice when she said, "I want to do something daring before I die, Olivia."

"Are you planning to die soon?" She teased.

"No, but it could happen tomorrow. You just never know when. I want to live today, Olivia!"

"Francesca! You're serious?"

"Yes, I am. I am tired of my boring, mundane everyday life. I want to change it."

"In what way?"

"Every way."

"How do you plan to do that?"

"I'm not sure yet. But one thing *is* for sure, I want *different*! I want something fantastic, something wonderful to think about while I sit in the nursing home, when I'm old and all gummy, staring stupefied into space."

Olivia laughed. "What's wrong? I thought you were happy. You're always so positive, a model of strength."

"That's because I settled for less. I've never demanded the best for myself, not really. In a way, I guess I didn't believe I deserved it, but now I do, Olivia. I want excitement in my life; so much that it will make me delirious."

"What brought all this about?"

"Ben and Julia."

"What? How?"

"They were offered a chance of a lifetime and ran with it, which made me think about my own life, and what I'm doing with it…not much I can tell you."

Olivia raised her eyebrows in surprise, "You've raised a family and…"

"Oh, I know," Francesca said, dismissing it with a wave of her hand. "That's not what I am talking about. It's about what I'm doing – oh, I mean, not doing now. I'm free to do whatever I want, but I'm not doing anything exciting. I'm just existing, Olivia. The highlight in my life at the moment is this place."

"What about, is it Mark, Mark Cooper, you're seeing?" Francesca nodded.

"Well, what about him? Isn't he important to you, to your future?"

"Mark is a sweet guy, but I don't think he's my future."

"Because?"

"I don't think he really loves me. He says he does, but his actions tell me differently. He doesn't make me feel loved. It's the little things that really tell the true story, Olivia. He's sweet and kind, but he doesn't feel the need for us to be in contact every day. He says he's not an exhibitionist and having to declare his feelings to someone all the time would be too demanding! To SOMEONE! Who the hell am I to him then?"

"Oh Francesca, I'm so sorry. You're a beautiful woman and you deserve better than that."

"I know I deserve better than that, Olivia. I'm finally beginning to understand my worth, as a woman and as a person. Something I failed to understand in my youth."

"I'm sure other people would have told you that you're beautiful."

"Yes, some have, but I didn't take any of that seriously. I thought the men who told me were just spinning me a line, and friends were being kind," she laughed, shrugging. "I had no idea they were actually stating a fact. I guess that sounds big-headed of me, but I'm just discovering myself, and I like this person. In the summer of my life, it was about my giving to everyone else, and since I'm heading towards autumn, it's going to be all about me for a change," Francesca declared. "You're a beautiful woman too Olivia and deservedly, Anton treated you like a princess. Mark should treasure me, but he doesn't. He's far too complacent; his actions today will determine whether we have a tomorrow, which looks highly unlikely."

"Have you told him how you feel? Perhaps ..."

Francesca shook her head interrupting, "No, no, Olivia, it's no use. I hear loud and clear what Mark means. He's adamant. I don't want to manipulate the way he thinks. It has to be natural from his heart. I know I'm worth it. But if Mark doesn't think I am, then we shouldn't be together. Olivia, I want PASSION in my life. I know what that's like. I had it once and it was f-a-b-u-l-o-u-s."

"Ooooh! Secrets...mmm." Olivia's dark eyes sparkled with curiosity.

"Mmm," Francesca smiled provocatively, "and what a delicious secret it is, my friend."

"Do tell," Olivia mischievously grinned.

"Well, about eighteen months ago I was out with the girls. It was only supposed to be dinner, but Nicky and some of the others wanted to visit Marlo's afterwards. The club was full that night; lights flashing in tempo with very loud, orgy music. The place was dingy and reeked of stale alcohol, perfume and sweaty bodies. I really wasn't interested in being there. If I hadn't been the designated driver, I would have left. I could barely see. It took a while for my eyes to adjust to the shadowy silhouettes under strobe lighting. When I could finally see, I got an eye-full of a gorgeous hunk of a man dancing the rumba with a cute blonde. I was mesmerised with the way he moved. After a while he looked up and noticed me watching him. He let go of the blonde and provocatively danced over to me with his hand outstretched, beckoning me to come to him. I couldn't resist, Olivia. *Oh my gawd!* I melted into his arms. He was the most sensual man that I'd ever known. When we danced, it was magical, as if we were one entity. All my inhibitions simply vanished. Ahhh! What absolute pleasure!"

Francesca ran her hands through her hair and twirled in a dance step, stopping in front of Olivia. "And that, my friend," Francesca gushed, "was the beginning of a six month affair of sheer pleasure and absolute passion."

Olivia was surprised, but not shocked, and was eager to know more.

"What brought the relationship to an end?"

A flicker of sadness flashed into Francesca's eyes. "It was complicated, Olivia. Jake Thurston was eight years my junior, very handsome and – black."

"Oh," Olivia said softly, resting a gentle hand on Francesca's arm. "No one can erase your memories, sweetie. Hold on tight to them, they can be a powerful tonic when you need it."

Francesca smiled knowingly at Olivia, and then as she began preparing the next day's menu. She worked on autopilot; memories of her time with Jake flooded her mind – *'she was with him and could feel his muscular frame against her lean body; his skin cool and smooth, his scent intoxicating, clinging to each other with such uncertainty, afraid that if either let go they would evaporate into thin air; a lifetime greedily absorbed into what little time they had; inhibition dissolved as their bodies entwined, exploring and enjoying a sublime obsession.'*

An appreciative smile warmed Francesca's spirit, as her thoughts drifted back to the evening she was driving home from one of her girl's-night-out.

Her mobile was ringing.
'Hello'
'Where are you?'
'Jake? Where are you?

'*Waiting for you.*'
'*Where?*'
'*At your place. I'm inside.*'
'*What?*" She laughed, '*How did you get in?*'
'*Through your bedroom window, I wanted to surprise you. I've come to ravish you.*'

She laughed, '*You're a bit sure of yourself, aren't you? What if I was with another man? Huh? What then?*'

'*I'd just throw him out, and then I'd make you forget him...*'

'*Ooooo, my sexy cave man, I'll be there in a minute. I'm just turning into my street.*'

When Francesca opened her front door, she found Jake standing in her lounge room, stark naked and thought what a pity Michelangelo hadn't seen Jake before he created his David. Jake was perfect. They walked slowly towards each other. '*Hello,*' he said, in his deep throaty way, '*I've been waiting for you.*'

She fell into his arms, '*I'm all yours.*'

Francesca screamed inwardly while furiously chopping onions, '*I want it again. I want to feel alive with every fibre of my being. I don't want second best anymore,*' recalling the way Jake looked at her and how he cherished her. The pride in his eyes when he looked at her and the way he claimed her as his woman when in public; leaning across the restaurant table, holding her face in his hands as he planted a kiss on the tip of her nose.

Olivia popped her head through the doorway, interrupting Francesca's thoughts, "Francesca,"

"Yes?"

"Got a minute?"

"Not now, Olivia, I've got heaps to do."

"I'll take care of that," Olivia said, undoing Francesca's apron, "I'm not expecting we'll be busy this late in the afternoon. Madison and Ali are here. I want you to take some time out for yourself."

Francesca responded with an awkward smile, "Yes, I think I will. Thanks Olivia, I might be coming down with something, I've got a massive headache. See you in the morning."

16

Mark Cooper sat on the edge of Francesca's bed, nursing a towel, facecloth and a bowl of ice water. "How are you feeling, darling?" He asked trying to conceal his concern, gently pushing back damp honey-blond hair away from her face.

Francesca tried to muster up a smile, "Awful," was all she could say before drifting back to sleep. Mark slipped the facecloth into the water, swirled it around, squeezed out the excess water, folded the cloth in half and then tenderly laid it upon Francesca's forehead. He did that several times trying to obliterate a myriad of tiny perspiration beads that refused to dissolve. He sat a vigilant watch throughout the night, making sure Francesca was comfortable.

While she was sleeping, he studied her lovely features and his heart suddenly skipped a beat, giving rise to every protective instinct in him. At that moment, it hit him how much Francesca meant to him. *'I love her,'* he was thinking. *'Yes, I really do. I can't ever recall feeling this way about anyone before. She looks so vulnerable – she's beautiful.'*

He gently brushed her cheek with the tip of his lips, and then laid down beside her. Exhaustion demanded that he sleep, but his eyes would not close; his thoughts were anxiety-driven. All he could do was stare at the ceiling, thinking about whether he should take Francesca to hospital.

'Dragging her out of a warm bed in the middle of the night might make things worse. Francesca said it was just a touch of the flu and would be fine in the morning, when she called to cancel our date. I wish I knew what to do. She looks so ill.'

Francesca's flushed cheeks told Mark the fever had not yet broken. He got up from the bed slowly so as not to disturb her and carried the bowl to the kitchen and refilled it with ice-water. Francesca stirred and mumbled something incoherent while Mark bathed her.

"It's ok, honey, It's ok," Mark whispered, "I'm here taking care of you."

Daylight filtering through the chiffon curtains woke Francesca. She ached all over, but felt much better than she had the day before. Slowly turning over, Francesca found Mark still dressed, curled up beside her. He looked a crumpled mess. Her movement startled him, "What? What? I'm here, are you alright? Can I get you anything? How are you feeling?"

Francesca laughed. She had never seen Mark in such disarray or confusion. Mark the accountant, the methodical and orderly man in a spin, *'Well that's something one wouldn't see every day'*.

"You well may laugh, Francesca, but I was worried sick. I didn't know what to do. If, if something should have happened to you, I ..."

"Shhh! Come here, I'm sorry," she said, holding him and pacifying him as if he were a child, "I had no idea you cared that much."

"Well," he said sheepishly, "neither had I, until I saw you so ill. I love you, Francesca."

The depth of Mark's sincerity surprised Francesca and she held him tighter. Everything changed between them in that moment. "I guess, at first, it was the great sex that kept me coming back," Mark confessed, and Francesca immediately smiled, thinking about Jake.

"We do have *great* sex, darling," he confessed, with a touch of arrogance, kissing the tip of Francesca's nose. "But really, it's more than that – I think about you all the time. I guess it was rather insensitive of me to think it unnecessary to call you or text you several times a day. I feel that you're with me every moment of the day, here," Mark patted his chest, "in my heart. I just assumed it was the same for you. Oh," he sighed, "perhaps women need more, I have no idea what women's needs are but I do want to understand what you need, darling."

Francesca began to weep.

"Hey hey my darling, why the tears?"

"I almost made the biggest mistake of my life."

"What do you mean?"

"I was about to end our relationship because I thought you didn't love me."

"Huh, I wouldn't have given up so easily, Francesca," Mark said seriously, holding her tighter, "I would have followed you to the end of the earth." He released his grip and looked into her eyes, "Where were you going?"

"Europe."

"Hmmm, good choice. We could go together, say on our honeymoon?"

"Pass the aspirin and the glass of water. I want a clear head when we celebrate after we shower," she smiled, provocatively.

Petting Francesca's neck, Mark asked, "How do you feel right now?"

"Great!"

"Then let's celebrate!" He yelled and she squealed with delight.

Two days later, Francesca bounced into the café. Her contagious joy was written all over her face. She hugged Olivia hello, "Oh Olivia, I'm soooo happy" she sang, "Mark's my champion. He nursed me back to health – among other things." she said, grinning shamelessly.

"So Europe is out?"

"Oh no, we're going there together, on our honeymoon!" Olivia's hands shot up to her mouth and her eyes widened in delight. "That's wonderful," she shouted. "I'm so happy for you, sweetie. Congratulations! We have to celebrate. I'll call the girls. Ali, Madison!"

They both came running to the kitchen and found Francesca and Olivia jumping around the room like dizzy teenagers. The younger women looked puzzled, "What's up? Have you two taken a hit of something?" Ali shouted over their laughter.

"What?" They both said in unison, coming to a standstill, "A what?"

"Nothing, forget it. What's going on?"

"Francesca and Mark are engaged."

"Wow, now that's really cool, Francesca, congratulations. I guess the party will be here? Olivia is teaching me all sorts of wonderful dishes, and I am learning authentic Italian cuisine from Gino, as well." Ali beamed with pride.

Olivia and Gino, the chef and owner of *Luci d'Italian* restaurant, have been friends since childhood. Olivia discussed

Ali's dilemma, regarding her not wanting to leave the Bay to do a chef's course, with Gino. Between them they devised a feasible plan for Ali to remain in the Bay and still do the course; Ali would become Gino's apprentice.

"Your engagement party is my gift to you and Mark." Olivia announced.

"And I'm cooking," Ali said enthusiastically.

"All you have to do is work out a date," Olivia said.

Three weeks later, Mark and Francesca's family and friends filled the transformed café, decked out in hundreds of fairy lights and dozens of candles flickering in the warm evening breeze, casting shadowy figures dancing around the room. Large trestle tables at the back of the room, covered with crisp white tablecloths, were laden with smorgasbord delights, while the jukebox worked overtime playing everybody's favourites; merriment filled the air.

Mid-evening, Mark gently tapped a spoon against his glass, calling everyone's attention, "Everyone! Hello! Can I have a moment please?" The jukebox was turned off and voices lowered to a murmur. "Thank you," he said laughing nervously, "This won't take long," and went on to thank everyone involved in the celebrations. "Apart from this evening being so amazing, I would say this is the best day of my life." He paused to smile lovingly at Francesca, "because it has taken me a long time to get this gorgeous woman to say, 'yes'. I feel very privileged that she has, and I am most eager to make my beautiful fiancé, my wife." Mark smiled broadly at the applause and even gave a little bow, feeling more than confident his speech was well received.

Nicky Porter sidled up to Olivia and handed her a glass of red wine. "Well," she said raising her glass, "the gang's all here, and then some. It's a great night, Olivia. You, Ali and Madison have really out-done yourselves," and tipped her glass against Olivia's.

Olivia smiled. "Thanks, Nic. Yes, it's a great night...just look at Francesca, she's glowing. I think Mark's ok." Olivia said rhetorically, giving her friend a questioning look.

Later in the evening, Ali joined Olivia. "What do you think of him?" she said, pointing to a dark-haired young man across the room.

"Where, love? What am I looking at?"

"That gorgeous guy standing by the door. What do you think?"

"Who for, love? You or for me?" Olivia teased.

"For meee," Ali said, in mocked indignation.

"Hmm, he seems ok, n-i-c-e looking, tall. Ahhh and Italian." Olivia winked.

"He's from Rome. He's Gino's nephew and he works at the restaurant, too."

"Does he have a name?"

"Pasquale Melano. He has asked me to have dinner with him Saturday night."

"Well, are you going?"

"I am." Ali said, giving Olivia a wicked smile as she sashayed back to her new beau's side.

17

On her day off, Ali went to Lilly's salon. No one had prepared her for what she would encounter when she walked through the door: fairy lights, pale-pink walls, large gold-filigree mirrors. In front of all that ostentatious gold filigree stood mint-green, vinyl chairs. Pipe music and a constellation mix of birdlife and forest sounds discreetly played in the background. Everything in the place either twinkled or sparkled, even Lilly and her assistant, Katie, who had just wandered out of the back room carrying mint coloured towels, as Ali came in. Katie was wearing the same slim-fitting, pink button-front dress and matching slip on high-heels, and mint-green, chiffon scarf around her blonde bouffant, as Lilly. The women look like identical twins.

Lilly greeted Ali warmly. "It's lovely to finally meet you, Ali," she said, in a soft, high musical intonation, "Maddie talks about you all the time," she beamed. Before Ali could respond, Lilly was leading her to one of the mint chairs. "There we are," she said, gently pushing Ali into the chair. "Now, from what Maddie tells me, you want to maintain your hair extensions, right?" Lilly asked, lifting handfuls of Ali's hair and moving it every which-way. "Hmm, I must say these are beautiful extensions. Maddie also mentioned that the other hairdressers attached these?"

Ali nodded. "Yes, they did. I'm happy with my hair, but I think it's time for a change."

Lilly smiled. "I understand." Tapping Ali gently on the arm. "Now, the question is. What style would you like?"

Ali thought for a moment, and then said, "Maddie said you're the best stylist in town. So since you're the best, I'll leave it up to you to decide a style for me. My fate is in your hands, Lilly." Ali grinned when Lilly's face lit up like a beacon.

"I know just the cut for you," she said, hardly containing her excitement, "Err, that's if you agree to my cutting your hair?"

"As I said, Lilly, I'm in your hands."

Two hours later, Ali left the salon sporting a layered razor cut, a soft and feminine style that would allow her to morph her shiny ebony curls into several different styles. Although Ali loved her new, short and sassy look, she was feeling a little nervous that Pasquale might not. She liked him and she wanted to please him.

Before she went home, Ali stopped by the café. She found Olivia taking advantage of the late afternoon lull by tidying up behind the counter. Olivia glanced up when Ali came in, but didn't recognise her in her haste to put things back in place,

"It's not polite to ignore your friends, Olivia."

"Wow, you look amazing! Lilly's place?"

"Yep!" Ali smiled, touching her hair. "More like fairyland than a salon."

"Lilly's different, but she's genuinely a kind and gentle soul."

"I can't disagree with that."

"When's your big date with Pasquale?"

"Tomorrow night. I hope he likes my new look but I'll see him in the morning at the restaurant."

"Well, if he doesn't, then he isn't the right man for you."

The male staff, with the exception of Pasquale, wolf-whistled when Ali arrived at the restaurant. Pasquale smiled at Ali when she looked directly at him, but his black eyes were cold. He dashed away from the bench and rushed up to her pecking her roughly on the cheek.

"You cut your beautiful hair," he said, in his thick Italian accent. Ali nodded with uncertainty. "Long hair betta, but this is ok." He responded, with a hint of dominance, touching her hair. He then said with authority, "Come Cara, we work."

Unbeknown to Ali, Jonathan and Harry were lurking in the shadows of the alfresco café across the street from *Luci d'Italian*, watching her. They had been discreetly stalking her for months, vowing revenge when their obvious absence from the Corner Café was ignored. Jonathan's hatred festered to the extent that he repeatedly chanted, "I'll destroy that *junkie* for humiliating me if it's the last thing I do!"

While he waited patiently for his time of retribution against Ali, Jonathan took every opportunity to satirically undermine the Corner Café to his tourist clients, making snide, provocative comments about how some of their customers fell ill after dining there, and that a *drug addict* worked there.

"One has to be so careful these days, where one goes," he cooed, in his feminine, thespian alto while he flitted about styling the client's hair. "One could so easily catch a deadly disease, and poof!" He would say with a flick of his hand, "one could die!"

By the time the client had left the salon, he or she would be filled with enough dread to avoid the café. But there were a few who were curious and wanted to see what the place was really like, regardless of the risk.

One woman, showing off in front of her friends, stretched her curiosity to the point of being rude by asking, when Olivia took their orders, if the rumours about the café were true. When Olivia's brows knitted together and her eyes narrowed, the woman knew she had said the wrong thing.

"What rumours?"

The woman stammered, "Aah…that a drug-addict works here and …"

Olivia snatched the menus from the woman and her friends' hands before she could utter another word and said, "Sorry, the kitchen is closed," and walked away.

The women sat there sniggering and laughing quietly making no attempt to leave, until Anton stood beside them; a chill like nothing any of them had experienced before encompassed them. They then almost fell over each other scurrying towards the door.

Olivia was livid and ripped off her apron on the way to the kitchen. "I'm going to give those two a piece of my mind," she barked, utterly confused by the behaviour of her former friends. Francesca and Madison looked at Olivia and asked what had happened, but she did not seem to hear them.

"You'd be wasting your breath, darling," Anton whispered in her ear.

"They'll get their dues."

As Olivia's anger subsided, Francesca's question penetrated her brain.

"What? Oh, nothing, just a couple of nasty customers, that's all."

Both Francesca and Madison knew there was more to it than that. They saw the anger blazing in Olivia's eyes. It was not her nature to be angered; she is kind and generous to a fault and neither of them had seen her behave like that, ever.

Once Olivia calmed down, she faced Francesca as if nothing had happened and asked, "Have you set a date for the wedding, love? It's been months since the engagement party. What are you waiting for?"

Francesca shrugged nonchalantly and glanced over at Madison and raised her eyebrows. Madison shrugged and carried on working.

"Not yet, Olivia, I'm getting around to it. Maybe we'll discuss it tonight. Mark rang from his office this morning, asking if I wanted to go out for dinner."

"That sounds romantic," Olivia smiled warmly. "Where's he taking you?"

"Luci d'Italian."

18

Mark had arranged to meet Francesca at the restaurant. As she drove into the car park, she could see him through the restaurant's huge feature window. He was sitting at the bar heavily engaged in conversation with a twenty-something waitress and, by his body language, he seemed very interested in her. Although Francesca felt betrayed, she also felt relieved, finally understanding why she could not commit to a wedding date.

Mark jumped up the instant he saw Francesca come in and rushed to her side, planting a kiss on her cheek.

"Hello, sweetheart," he chirped innocuously. "You look smashing as usual," and led her to their table. He pulled out the chair, bowed and said, "Madame." Francesca smiled her thanks and sat down.

"Have you been waiting long?" She casually asked.

"No, I arrived only few minutes before you."

'He sounds so convincing, I would have believed him,' she thought, 'if I hadn't have seen him have that drink. I wonder how many other times he's lied to me.'

"How was your day?" She asked sweetly. "I would have been here sooner, but I got caught up at work."

"Just as long …"

"Excuse me," the waitress Mark was flirting with earlier, gushed. "Are you ready to order?"

Francesca turned to the girl. "Is Gino here? I would like to say hello to him."

"Gino isn't here tonight," she replied smiling at Mark.

"Oh," Francesca said, feeling a little disappointed. *'Everything so far about this evening was disappointing, arriving late and finding my fiancé chatting up the waitress. What else?'* She wondered.

Over dinner, Mark brought up the wedding. "Darling, have you decided on a date yet?"

"Why? What's the rush?"

Mark nearly choked on his food. "Rush!" He barked and heads turned.

"Shhhh! You don't have to shout."

He leaned forward and lowered his voice. "Honey, it's been almost a year. We have things to sort out. Our properties. Where we live."

While Mark was speaking, Francesca noticed he had one eye on the waitress and realised she did not care. She looked down at her left hand and studied the large diamond ring on her finger, then considered how her impeccably dressed, debonair fiancé was not giving her one hundred per cent. *'I can't marry him.'*

Mark's face turned ashen when Francesca slowly removed the ring and handed it to him.

"There," she whispered. "I've fixed the date. Never! Give it to the waitress you've been ogling since you arrived."

"But…"

She stood up. "No buts Mark – that's it – oh, and the sex wasn't that great for me. I'll send you your things. DON'T CALL ME!"

As Francesca walked calmly out of the restaurant, smiling vivaciously and feeling totally liberated, she caught sight of her shapely reflection in the mirror at the entrance and liked what she saw and thought, *'I was a fool for sending Jake away. That gorgeous man loved me; our age difference didn't matter to him.'*

The minute Francesca arrived home, she immediately went about the house calmly gathering up Mark's belongings, books, his mug, tailor-made suits and shirts, hand-made Italian shoes, his Beatles album collection, which she could not stand (Francesca was a Pink Floyd fan) his runners and so on, and packed them neatly into cardboard boxes. She got more than she had bargained for when she picked up off the floor, the screwed-up piece of paper that fell out of Mark's suit jacket when it slid off the hanger. Thinking it was rubbish, she was about to throw it away, then stopped and slowly unravelled it. Her eyes filled with horror as she silently mouthed the words on the paper. *'Mark, honey, once is not enough with a guy like you...you know how the song goes. See you soon??? Lola.'*

A rage burned deep inside Francesca's belly, her heart raced so hard that she trembled as she upended the precisely packed contents of all the boxes, furiously shaking them several times to make sure there was nothing left inside. She then scooped up the items and savagely jammed them all into huge, plastic garbage bags, tied a knot and tossed them aside, to be taken to charity. Lola's note was sent to Mark with a covering note of her own. *"Your things went to charity: score settled! DON"T EVER COME NEAR ME AGAIN!"*

The following day Francesca called a cleaning company and made an appointment to have her home fumigated from top to bottom, and then cheerfully drove to the café, feeling that since the matter was finished, as far as she was concerned, there was no point going into details when she told her friends that she and Mark were no long together. *'Mark wasn't that important.'*

"You what?" Olivia was not sure whether to laugh or cry as she studied Francesca a moment, searching for some signs of regret and saw none, fully aware that she had left out the part about finding Lola's note. Anton had forewarned Olivia about Mark's infidelity some months prior, and cautioned her not to interfere.

'I cannot stand by and do nothing. Francesca's a dear friend,' challenged Olivia, as her lovely features contorted, imagining her friend's pain.

'Everything has to run its course, my love. Francesca is strong, she'll work it out herself. Francesca needs to skipper her own ship. Promise me you won't interfere?' Olivia reluctantly agreed.

"Oh, sweetie, I'm so sorry. Are you ok?"

"Yes, I am. I'm over it, Olivia. I'm now ready to get on with whatever life has to offer. At least now I know who and what he is...I just couldn't get past that nagging feeling...you cannot beat good old-fashion intuition."

"No, you can't!" a voice came from behind.

"Julia!" Olivia and Francesca cried in unison, turning simultaneously and stared at the 165 cm, linen clad redhead, who more resembled an international model than the earthy woman she used to be.

"Where on earth did you come from?" barked Olivia. "Oh, of course, I know where you came from," Olivia laughed hollowly, craning her neck looking over Julia's shoulder.

"Where's Ben? What are you doing here? Not that I'm not glad to see you, darling. Why didn't you call?"

"Oh Mum," Julia's shoulders drooped, "I'm sorry. I didn't think. I, I didn't …" she burst into a flood of tears before finishing the sentence. "I've left Ben."

"What?" Olivia was consoling her. "No, no you couldn't have. You two are, were so, so in love. No. Why?"

"I couldn't take any more. She, Ben's secretary, Maria, came between us. She's beautiful, Mum. I can't compete with her so I just left. Ben doesn't know, well, I guess he would know by now. I left him a note," Julia sniffed.

"Has my son cheated with…?"

"NO! No, I just couldn't get near Ben during the day. He spent so much of his time locked up in office for one conference after another. I left messages, but he never seemed to get them. That, that witch intercepted them every time. She's had her sights on Ben from the first day we met."

"Honey, it takes two to have an affair. It wouldn't matter how beautiful this woman is, Ben's in love with you, his wife. Have you talked to Ben about all of this?"

"He's been so busy from the moment we arrived in Rome. Every night he'd come home late and depleted. Some nights he's asleep before he's eaten. Besides, I don't know how to. Ben will think I'm being petty and jealous. He can't see that she's manipulating him. She's *Miss Wonderful*, blah, blah. How can I compete with that when all I do is sightsee and read my time away; I feel so inadequate without a job. We've lost each other; Mum, that job has stolen my husband and our life."

Francesca went quietly about filling orders, while Julia and Olivia sat huddled together in the corner of the kitchen talking. In the middle of their conversation, Julia's mobile rang.

"Hello."

"What are you doing? I'm out of my mind with worry." Ben barked, and Julia burst into tears again. Olivia took the phone from her and said, "Ben, its Mum."

"Mum, what the hell's going on? Julia's left and I don't understand why. Did she tell you?"

"Darling, your wife feels your job has stolen you away from her, and that she cannot compete with it. And then there's the matter of Maria, Ben?"

"Please give the phone to Jules, Mum." Olivia passed the mobile to Julia.

"Ben?"

"I've got a few things to tidy up round here, and then I'll be on the first plane home, ok, baby? We'll talk then. Ok?"

"Ok. Bye."

Olivia thought Julia's eyes sparked when she glanced over at her and said, "Ben's coming home."

Francesca placed two coffees in front of them. "Here, I think both of you could do with this right now," and then joined Ali and Madison in the dining room. As she was leaving the kitchen, Francesca heard Julia telling Olivia: "Italy would have been wonderful, if only Ben had been with me … " It was at that moment Francesca knew she was going to Italy.

19

The following day Francesca's mind was on her Italian holiday, and how she would break the news to Olivia that she was definitely going. Unbeknown to her, Olivia already knew and had asked Julia to fill in while Francesca was away, so she would be free to leave right away.

"Strike while the iron is hot, love," Olivia said, "Go, girl, go and have the time of your life and, perhaps, you just might find the man of your dreams."

Francesca was delirious with excitement. "Just do it, like the sign says. Ok. I'm going to – just do it! I'm calling the travel agent right now."

A half an hour on the phone and everything was in place. Francesca turned to Olivia amazed, "I leave Friday night. Can you believe it? Oh my, Olivia, I can't believe I've done it. I'm going to Italy! I've wanted to do that for such a long time, and now it's finally happening. Three days. Ha! I've got three days to pack."

"Buona sera, Mama. Buona sera, Francesca."

"Ben!"

"There's never a dull moment around here, that's for sure," Olivia laughed, "Come here and give your mother a hug."

"Buona sera, Ben. I'm leaving Friday night for Rome."

"Really?"

"I sure am."

"Wonderful! I'll arrange for Marco Amici to meet you at the airport, and show you around the city if you like? It can be a bit tricky in Rome on your own when you don't know the language."

"Fantastic, thanks, Ben! I won't say no to that. We can talk later after you get a few things sorted out here," she smiled. "See you later, Olivia. Talk soon, Ben."

"Ok Francesca. Now Mum," Ben turned to Olivia, "Where's Jules? I thought she'd be here with you. I wanted to surprise her."

"Julia would have been, darling, but she wasn't feeling well this morning. I suggested she stay in bed. I guess she's still recovering from the flight, that's a long trip home. How about you, sweetheart? You must be drained, too."

"I'm ok. I managed to sleep all the way. The company jet is very comfortable. If you don't mind, Mum, I would like to go and see Jules."

Ben could hear Julia throwing her heart up in the bathroom, from the front door. He heard the toilet flush and the tap run. Julia came staggering out of the bathroom, wiping her face with a wet face washer. She jumped backwards when Ben spoke.

"Honey! What's wrong?"

"Ben! You almost scared the life out of me. I thought you were going to call. I feel rotten. I want to die." She fell into his arms. "I don't know what is making me so ill," she moaned like a miserable child. "Maybe something I ate on the plane. I felt unwell all the way home. Maybe I'm just overtired from the flight. I don't know. Come and lie down beside me. I'll be better soon."

Just as they settled on the bed, Julia was up again and running to the bathroom. When it happened a third time, Ben jumped up. "That's it. You're going to the hospital."

Julia was about to protest, but another bout of sickness sent her back to the bathroom. She came out spent. "Ok, I give in, I'll go."

They had a long wait in the emergency room. Ben took that time to remind Julia of their promise to one another. "What about our song, Jules? "If I should fall behind, you'll wait for me: we promised to wait for each other. Remember? I would never betray you, never."

"I'm sorry, darling, I wasn't thinking. I felt shut out. I think that's why I'm so sick. Everything has upset me so much. I was so, so lonely and sad without you. We hardly saw each other and, and Maria – that witch – she wouldn't ..."

"It's ok now." Ben said soothing her, not wanting to get into the Maria thing. He was angry enough with himself for being so blind, for not seeing how she manipulated the whole thing, intercepting Julia's messages and making excuses to keep him longer than necessary at the office, arranging intimate dinners while they worked on projects.

"Everything's sorted out now, honey."

"Are we going back to Italy?"

"No, baby, I quit."

"You quit? Oh, Ben."

"We're more important than that job. I still have the practice, and I won't be working the hours I did in Rome. I can delegate most of the work to the other guys. Our marriage, you, we come first ..." As Julia listened, she snuggled into Ben's chest, feeling more secure.

"Mrs Julia Rossetti," the doctor called.

After examining Julia thoroughly, the doctor asked her all sorts of questions she thought did not seem relevant to her condition, jet-lag. Out of the blue, he said, "Have you considered starting a family?"

"What?" they both said, in disbelief.

"Are we pregnant?" Julia asked, looking over at Ben who was grinning like a fool

"Four months."

Once again the Corner Café was preparing for another celebration; to toast Ben and Julia's good news and to Francesca's Italian holiday.

As promised, Ben made arrangements for one of his friends to meet Francesca at Fiumicino Airport and to give her a personal tour of Rome.

"Oh, Ben, you're wonderful. Thank you so much."

"What are your plans, Francesca?" Julia asked.

First stop Kuala Lumpur, two days there, then a couple of days in Rome and then I'm taking a train to Tuscany. I would like to stay a couple of weeks in the Creti region near Cortona. I can do day trips to Florence from there. Then to Venice for a few days; and back to Rome for another week."

"You will love Tuscany, the countryside is so beautiful," Julia said. "While Ben was chained to his desk," she teased, gripping hold of his arm, laughing, "I did a lot of travelling around the country. I fell in love with Tuscany. It's out of this world."

"I'm hoping to have a relaxing stay there, after what I imagine will be a hectic sightseeing trip around Rome," Francesca responded, hardly believing this was actually happening. "Casa Bellavista looks like the perfect place to do just that."

"I'm sure you will have a wonderful time, Francesca." Ben said, "Marco is a good friend of mine, he'll look after you. If you need anything, just let him know."

Francesca smiled broadly, wondering when she will wake up and find that it is all just a dream.

"I can't thank you both enough."

"Just have a great time." Ben said, hugging her.

"Oh, I intend to," she said mischievously, hugging Julia. "Now, you both must take care also."

20

While Ali worked the midday shift with Olivia, she said, "I really hope Francesca meets a really cool Italian and has a romantic holiday."

Olivia glanced sideways at her and smiled, "Ah, you're such a romantic now that you're in love. You desire the world to be in love too."

"Who said I'm in love?"

"It's written all over your face."

Ignoring the remark, Ali asked Olivia if she could ask her a personal question.

"Well that depends on the question, ask and I'll see."

"The day of Tom's accident, you said Anton was with you. Do you remember? What did you mean by that?"

"Yes, I remember clearly, love. Well, it's a long story," Olivia sighed, "but I'll give you the short version. I haven't discussed this before, not even with Ben or Julia. I know this may seem like a cliché, but my wedding day was the happiest day of my life, giving birth to Ben was the second happiest day and Anton is the love of my life and I am his. He promised we'd be together – forever, and then he died suddenly of a heart attack. I was devastated and angry, he had broken his promise – he left me. I was inconsolable. I wanted to die too. I felt empty. Then one day he came back and told me that he doesn't break promises that everything will be ok, and it was. I wasn't sure whether or not he was a figment of my imagination I didn't care because I can see him, hear him and talk to him every day, I'm happy!"

"Wow, that's cool Olivia, really cool and romantic." There was a sparkle in Ali's eyes as she realised why Ben looked so familiar when she first met him.

Olivia looked over Ali's shoulder, "He's here all the time."

"Ben looks like Anton, doesn't he?"

"Why yes, he does. How did you know that?"

"I think I saw Anton sitting at the booth the day I applied for the job, but I thought it was a reflection in the window." Olivia nodded remembering. "You also know why I haven't contacted my family, don't you?"

"Yes, I do, Ali, but I assumed that one day you'd tell me yourself. Although I am genuinely interested, that day won't be today, sweetheart." Olivia said, and left the kitchen, telling Ali she wouldn't be long, when a man came in and sat down at the counter.

Olivia studied the tall handsome stranger for a moment. Since Madison was busy, she handed him a menu. After general pleasantries, she said, "I'll give you a minute and come back," and went to walk away.

"Excuse me, Ma'am, I'll have a coffee please and – I was wondering if you could tell me where I can find Francesca Cahill?"

Olivia turned back to face him, her dark eyes full of excitement, imagining Francesca's joy to know he came back.

"Are you Jake Thurston?"

"Francesca told you about me – about us?"

"She did. I'm Olivia."

"Where is she? Please, I have to talk to her."

"Francesca's gone to Italy, she left several days ago."

"With anyone?"

"She was alone, but who knows now," Olivia said, testing his reaction. "She's a lovely woman,"

"Francesca's a beautiful woman." Jake said, softening his voice, "Please tell Francesca I am looking for her …

21

Francesca's flight touched down at Kuala Lumpur around 5.30 am. The airport was deserted with the exception of new arrivals, a few ground staff and Customs officers. Francesca was one of the first to collect her baggage and go through Customs. The travel agent assured her a coach would be at the airport to take her and other passengers to the Concord Inn, but she was not sure where to wait. After asking for directions, Francesca was directed to a lift that took her to ground level, where she exited and walked out into the street; it was deserted. Or so she thought. Out of the corner of her eye something moved. She turned suddenly. Coming out of the shadows were two formidable, armed police officers in dark uniforms: One male and the other female. The male officer, tall, lean and handsome, stepped in front of his very attractive, female offsider. They both loomed over Francesca. Masking her fear, Francesca addressed the male officer and asked him where she could find the coach that would take her to the Concord Inn. He stepped closer; adjusting the semi-automatic weapon he was carrying said, "The coach will not be long. Wait inside."

'Yes sirree Bob,' she thought, *'I'm not going to argue with you.'*

Just minutes later, the coach arrived and collected Francesca and three other passengers. Francesca was dog-tired. All she wanted was a shower and sleep in a comfortable bed.

Noisy travellers passing by Francesca's room woke her. Frazzled and disoriented, she imagined she had overslept and dashed out of bed, showered and dressed, checked out, and caught the coach back to the airport. She even went through the rigmarole of checking in her luggage, only to be told she was a day early.

"Oh no," she moaned, "when's the next flight to Rome?"

"Your flight to Rome, Madam is leaving at 11.30 pm – tomorrow night. I can book your seat for you now, if you want me to do that for you. Then all you have to do is check in your luggage, when you come back tomorrow night. Ok?"

Once that was done, Francesca dragged herself and her luggage back downstairs and waited for the coach to take her back to her hotel. The coach driver gave her a big welcoming, questioning smile when she approached him. "Wrong night," she shrugged.

"Ok, ok tomorrow," he said, too polite to laugh.

The same thing happened when she entered the inn. The young man at the desk was very understanding and the staff said hello, as if she were a regular guest, and was shown back to her room, where she fell into bed.

At breakfast, Francesca met an Australian woman on her way home from Ireland. She suggested the best way to kill time was to do a day tour around the city. Another woman overheard their conversation and recommended the tour guide she had. Francesca contacted the guide and knocked down his price from one hundred and fifty dollars to one hundred dollars for a six hour tour.

A short time later, a shiny black car pulled up in front of the hotel. Francesca knew by the number plate it was her guide. He reached across and opened the front door, but she climbed in the back. He was a thirty-something, baby-faced man named Syaha who obviously enjoyed his job, happily chatting fast and furiously about places of interests with Francesca as he drove past, just as fast and furiously.

She did not have the heart to tell him that he was talking too fast for her to comprehend all of what he was saying. She was not that interested anyway. Italy was her focus. The tour was only a means of killing time. Francesca graciously smiled and nodded, doing her best to appear appreciative of the sights and wonders he pointed to, suggesting she take a photo of this or that magnificent sight. Her digital camera was full of images of tall buildings, gardens, the twin towers and of other places around the city. They explored the twin towers and enjoyed the panoramic view, and Francesca took more photos at Syaha's insistence.

After driving and then walking five exhausting hours around the city, Francesca wanted to find a café. "I have to stop for a coffee," she pleaded, and walked into a crowded mall. She offered to get Syaha one as well.

"Oh, no thank you," he said, "I am fasting."

Syaha sat with Francesca as she sipped at the bitter-tasting liquid, passed off as coffee while she watched the passing parade; the buzz of activity and the smell of food and incenses made her feel dizzy. She was ready to leave.

"I like your hair. It is very beautiful," she heard Syaha say over the top of the racket, and almost choked on the hot liquid. "Is it natural or with chemical?"

Francesca was beginning to feel uncomfortable, but said, "Some natural and some chemical," because he persisted.

"How old are you?" was his next question.

"Now Syaha, in my country a man never asks a woman her age."

"Thirty-something, maybe?"

She was annoyed and responded sternly, "Syaha, it is not polite to mention a woman's age," then quickly changed the subject. "Tell me about your family," she said in a lighter tone. "Do you have photographs of them?"

He pulled out his wallet and produced a group photograph of his pretty wife and two attractive children, a girl and a boy.

"You have a lovely family."

"Thank you, Ma'am, my culture allows me to have four wives," he announced proudly.

"That seems a lot of trouble for one man to handle."

He looked puzzled.

"Think about it. It would take a great deal of energy to spread yourself four ways, very difficult indeed. What if one of the wives was unhappy or jealous of the other wives or worse, what if all four wives were unhappy at the same time. What a mess that'd be? You'd have to be a very rich man to keep four wives happy. If you weren't a rich man, you'd have to work very hard, for the rest of your life, to keep all of your wives and all of your children fed and clothed. One wife is better. Life would be much simpler." Francesca smiled. "In my country only one wife is allowed. It's illegal to have more than one wife at a time – the man could end up in jail."

By the expression on Syaha's face, Francesca had given him plenty to think about. Her parting words to him were, "One wife is better."

He smiled warmly, waving goodbye. "Yes Ma'am."

Excitement for an unknown adventure began to give rise in Francesca the moment the aircraft landed at Leonardo De Vinci Airport. She went through Customs quickly and then wasted no time walking to the outer waiting area. She stepped aside for passengers rushing past, eager to get to their destinations to scan the sea of foreign faces looking for Marco Amici.

Through the mayhem, Francesca caught a glimpse of a 180 cm, well-built, attractive Italian dressed in a dark business suit, holding a card with her name, written in large, bold lettering, standing on the opposite side. Relieved to see the sign, she headed for the person holding it.

Marco Amici's eyes lit up when he saw a tall, elegant blonde walking towards him; Marco's dedication to his law profession had robbed him of a life, and his twelve-year marriage. Realising life was slipping by, he made a conscious effort to change things; and went as far as reading self-help books on how to rediscover himself. Francesca had also read many of the same sorts of books. Rose was the reader of the group, and was always talking about this or that book she found inspiring, so Francesca quietly went out and bought a copy. Otherwise, she would never have been brave enough to travel so far from home alone.

"Buon giornata, Marco Amici?" Francesca said, offering her hand.

"Ah si, Buon giornata, Signora Cahill, welcome to Roma."

"Thank you. It's Francesca," she said, delighted to have such an attractive guide.

'Hmm, I'm going to enjoy this holiday.'

Marco took Francesca's luggage from her, "I carry this please," he said. "You do not mind, we take train to Roma? Parking impossible everywhere, many things difficult in my country," Marco remarked, jerking his head upwards and clicking his tongue in disgust. He subconsciously did that every time he found something disagreeable, which was often. It amused Francesca how Marco had a love-hate relationship with Italy, frustrated with bureaucracy when trying to get the simplest of things done.

"Have you ever thought of living in another country?"

"Ah, si, every day, but as you see, I still here," he laughed.

Marco was fascinated with Francesca and observed her closely. To his embarrassment, he noticed that she was taking in the surroundings like an *inspector*.

"Ah, you see this beautiful city very dirty. It shameful, council do not care."

"Oh I wasn't. I…I was admiring the splendour of the buildings, imagining what had taken place here hundreds of years ago…how marvellous and romantic it all seems. But now that you've drawn my attention to it, the city is very dirty and, yes, it's a shame. But I'm sure tourists, like me, are only interested in the history and the splendid architecture."

"Ah si, what you like to do today? I am for your service."

"That's very kind of you to give up your time for me, but I don't want to keep you from your work."

"Ha," he said, waving his hand in the air and rolling his eyes, "work will be always. Not every day I have pleasure and company of beautiful lady to show my city."

Francesca was almost dead on her feet, after the long flight, but she did not want to break the momentum of the moment she was enjoying. *'Perhaps it would all end by evening,'* she was thinking, *'so why not seize the moment.'* She smiled warmly at him. "That sounds wonderful, Marco, but if you don't mind, I would like to freshen up first."

"Ah si, si, no rush.

22

At the far end of the counter Peter Bates, 180 cm tall, about mid-forties, was writing on a notepad when Ali appeared at the counter, startling him. "Want anything else?" She barked at him, stony-faced, smelling a copper.

"Yeah, love, another skinny cap and a piece of that chocolate fudge cake, thanks." He knew Ali had picked him. He also knew he had come to the right place.

In the background Nicky was saying, "Well, what's the latest with Francesca has anyone heard from her?"

"Olivia has all the news; she will be out in a minute." Rose said, lowering her voice to a whisper, "Mmmm, here she comes with lemon meringue pie."

"Haa! Working on our winter skin, eh?" Nicky teased.

"Si." Olivia said, placing the pie on the table in front of them.

"It sounds like our girl's having a marvellous time?" Rose chirped, wearing a cheeky grin.

"You could say that." Olivia said. "Francesca has sent you all postcards, and apparently this Marco is quite a man. I think she really likes him, and he is available."

The women were too involved in their conversation to notice Jake come in, and stand at the entrance listening. Peter Bates was also listening, fascinated and wondering who Francesca was. *'She seems to be a heartbreaker'*, he was thinking. *'By the look on the guy's face at the door, he wants to be more than her friend.'*

Olivia looked up just as Jake was leaving, her expression froze. "Oh no," she muttered under her breath and made a dash for the door, and caught it just before it closed behind him.

"Jake!" She called, but he kept walking.

"Wait a minute. I'm sorry. We …"

He stopped suddenly and turned around to face Olivia. "You didn't tell her, did you, Olivia?" His anger was driven by the ache in his heart. "Francesca doesn't know I'm here, does she, Olivia?"

"No Jake, I didn't tell her you were here because, well– because I know she would have cancelled the trip and come home. She's having a wonderful time. She deserves that much. I don't want to be the one to interrupt her holiday. Here, take it. It's her email address. Tell her yourself – or you could let her enjoy the rest of her holiday and wait until she returns."

"What if I lose her to that Italian, what's his name?"

"Marco."

"Right."

"Francesca isn't flighty, Jake, or the kind of woman to play games. So if there's something developing between her and Marco, it'll be real, but she isn't foolish enough to rush into anything."

Feeling defeated, Jake's shoulders drooped and he hung his head.

"I get the feeling you're still very important to her."

He lifted his head and stood taller. "Do you really think so, Olivia?"

"What I do think, Jake, is that love's a very strong emotion and it needs room to blossom. Understand what I'm saying?"

He nodded. "Let nature take its course?"

"That's right."

"Ok." Jake promised. "I'll call her when she gets home."

The women were clustered together, watching the scene between Jake and Olivia through the café window. They saw her wave him goodbye and turn around and come back inside.

"Is everything ok, Olivia?" Nicky asked. "That gorgeous man looks heartsick."

Olivia stood by the booth a moment, looking at her. "I hope so, kiddo, I certainly hope so. It's all in destiny's hands now."

23

In Rome, Marco waited patiently in the hotel lobby while Francesca was shown to her room. The porter opened the door and turned on the lights before he carried the bags in and placed them on a rack behind the door. As soon as he left, Francesca switched the lights off and drew back the heavy curtains, pushed opened the shutters and allowed the natural light to flood the room. She leaned out of the huge open window and felt the chill in the air, but the weather promised a glorious day. She looked up and down the narrow, cobblestone street. Vehicles and scooters were parked in rickety lines either side of the street, allowing little room for passing traffic. The street noise sounded hollow, and echoed upwards. The buildings across the street seemed impersonal and open to onlookers.

A half an hour later, Francesca, casually dressed in jeans, tee-shirt and flatties on her feet and carrying her linen jacket over her arm, was making her way back downstairs. Marco jumped to attention when he saw her, and said in his thick Italian accent that made every word he uttered sound like poetry. "Ah si, you good now?"

"I certainly am thank you."

"Hungry?" he asked with a questioning look.

"Famished."

"Ok, we eat, then we walking to city. Come, I find nice place".

Marco guided Francesca out of the hotel and down the street, navigating a path around parked cars, scooters, motorbikes and animal excrement.

"This would never be acceptable in Australia," Francesca said horrified, stepping aside to avoid the excrement. "We have regulations and fines to encourage people to take responsibility for their pets." She was equally amazed to see so many cats roaming freely around the city. "There must be hundreds of cats here. I adore cats, but this is ridiculous!"

"So many cats not good, but it is this way. We should have same law as Australia."

While walking the short distance to the restaurant, Francesca became acutely aware of screeching sirens and horns blasting aggressively. The noise was irritating and unrelenting. Arguments between taxi drivers around Termini Railway Station flared up out of the blue, drawing small crowds to further congest the footpath.

"You know, Marco," Francesca said flippantly, "your government could get very wealthy just by imposing parking fines and noise and pet pollution fines."

Marco's smooth forehead creased into several thick folds. "What you mean?"

"In Australia there are laws against all this," she explained, making a wide sweep of her arm.

"I've only been in Rome five minutes and already I'm so appreciative that I don't have to tolerate such aggression at home. I love Australia, it's a wonderful country. It may not have the history Italy has, but it is CLEAN and less aggressive, especially in Segal Bay, it's so peaceful."

Marco's smile faded, "You disappointment with Roma?"

Francesca came to a standstill; her eyes grew wide with surprise. "No! Rome is WONDERFUL! An ancient city, bursting with extraordinary history woven into a tapestry of modern culture! How could that be disappointing? I'm in awe that we're walking on cobblestones, the same cobblestones that people, hundreds of years before us, walked on, that alone is AMAZING!"

Marco lifted his head a little higher and stood a little straighter, as he began to see Rome through Francesca's eyes. As they continued walking, he slipped his arm in hers.

"I'm not saying everything in Australia is perfect, because it isn't," Francesca went on, "but judging by the near misses I've witnessed, just in this short space of time, as people try to cross these traffic-congested, chaotic roads and are almost rundown, I can safely say pedestrians in Australia are most definitely much safer crossing the street in our major cities than the pedestrians here in Rome. Nobody respects the road rules here, or perhaps there aren't any?"

They were still discussing the subject when they came up to a corner and were seemingly shouting at each other to be heard over the roar of the traffic noise and a gusty breeze. Although the pedestrian light was green, Marco vigilantly looked around before crossing. Francesca's foot was mid-air, about to step off the kerb when suddenly, from nowhere, a man on a scooter sped through the red light, blasting the horn, yelling abuse at her, as if she had no right to be there. Marco jerked her backwards by her arm, a split second before the rider sped past.

"Ah si, no manners I tell you," he shouted, clicking his tongue, rolling his eyes and waving his hands about like an eccentric maestro. "Be careful ..." he demanded, scolding Francesca as if she were a child.

"I didn't run the bloody light," she snapped back, "that idiot did. This is exactly what I'm talking about!"

Marco stepped backwards and took a deep breath. When he felt calmer he apologised, but continued lecturing Francesca about road safety at the restaurant while they ate. She sat back and observed him closely, her features softened and her frustration subsided when she realised Marco was not angry with her, just concerned for her safety.

In spite of its drawbacks, Rome intrigued Francesca; every step was a snapshot. She was twisting and turning every which-way, mesmerised by the wonders around her, capturing the experience on her digital camera. Tourists had bumped into her as they, too, gawked wide-eyed at architecture, old ruins and sculptures.

Francesca was amused, watching from afar, the many enervated, over-weight tourist groups, laden down with water bottles, jackets, bags and cameras, trailing behind marathon-runner type tour guides who periodically waved in the air, the long thin pole they carried with a coloured flag atop. The groups struggled breathlessly to keep the coloured flag in sight, so as not to get lost. They popped up when least expected and disappeared into buildings just as suddenly; looking very much like *Keystone Cops* in the silent movies. Upon each sighting she smiled and imagined marching band music playing, and then instantly stopping when they vanished into buildings or cathedrals.

By afternoon, Francesca and Marco had walked a great distance around the city. They window shopped famous designer stores, stopped at ancient ruins, crossed ancient bridges and even bravely ran the gauntlet several times to cross roads. They weaved their way through narrow streets that led them to the Spanish Steps, and then on to the Trevi Fountain, something of which, Francesca has had a romantic notion about for most of her life.

Marco chattered cheerfully to Francesca as they idly strolled up the narrow street leading to Trevi Fountain. She was not listening, but instead, images of her turning the corner and being magically drawn to the fountain's edge, ran rampant through her notoriously romantic mind. But before she was carried farther into her fantasy, a thunderous roar snapped her out of it, stopping her dead in her tracks, jerking on Marco's arm, alarming him.

"What's that noise?" She said, with a note of concern, "It's deafening?"

Marco's handsome features creased into tiny folds as he laughed, "The fountain, Cara, just around corner."

Bubbling over with great expectations, Francesca quickened her last few paces. She turned into Piazza Di Trevi and stood on the rise. Her eyes bulged in utter disbelief and her effervescent smile went flat. The scene before her played out like a United Nations Mardi Gras; the fountain was barely visible through the hundreds of global tourists, five rows thick, gathered around the fountain, taking photos, throwing in coins to make their traditional wish; to return to Rome. Clowns carrying colourful balloons were strolling aimlessly about while food and souvenir vendors loudly spruiked their wares as roving musicians played familiar Italian songs. The magic was gone. The illusion of romantic scenes portrayed in the movie classic, *Three Coins in the Fountain*, dissolved before her eyes.

Marco observed Francesca's reaction from the periphery of his vision.

"You disappointed si?" he asked.

"How did you know?"

"You wearing that face," he said seriously.

"What face?"

"The face you wearing at corner, where you nearly run over."

She felt uncomfortable that he could read her so well, then immediately saw the funny side of the situation and laughed.

"In the movie the fountain looks so different and wonderfully romantic. In reality, it looks nothing like that!"

"Ah, si Francesca, reality is truth. What you like, fairy tale or truth?"

"I just thought it'd be different, that's all, magical and romantic," she explained, feeling a little annoyed that he did not understand. "You're Italian!" she snapped, a little harder than she meant to. "I thought you of all people, would understand. Italians are supposed to be passionate and romantic …"

"I passionate, romantic also, but practical," he chipped.

"Practical is boring," she responded, turning away from him.

"You say I boring."

"No, no, of course not! Oh," she sighed, exasperated, as she turned and faced him. "Let's change the subject."

"Ok, we eat!" Marco declared, pointing ahead, directing her forward, and they began navigating their way through the crowd. They only walked a short distance up the street before they came across a restaurant they both agreed upon.

While perusing the menu, Francesca felt it prudent not to mention that although the food and wine on the menu looked appetising, they were indeed very expensive and she offered to pay her share of the bill before they ordered. Marco was aghast and horrified.

"The lady *never* pays!" He said, as if it were undignified of her to even suggest such a thing.

"Well, that custom may be acceptable for you, Marco, but I'm an independent woman who always pays her way, when she is dining with friends."

Marco raised his hand for her to stop, and said with determination, "You my guest, Francesca, we speak no more!"

Since pride sat firm in Marco's eyes, Francesca relented, deciding not to challenge him for the sake of her ego. To ease the mounting tension between them, Marco directed the conversation to Francesca's vacation plans.

"When you go to Tuscany?"

"I'm catching the Terontola-Cortona train tomorrow afternoon. I'm very excited about visiting Casa Bellavista," she smiled enthusiastically.

"I not know this place." Marco said, shrugging his shoulders, disappointed that she was leaving. "There is many lovely places to staying in Tuscany and countryside, so beautiful."

"Yes, I know. I've done my research. That's how I found Casa Bellavista. I was going to rent a car and see the sights, but I've since changed my mind. Sightseeing is so exhausting. I want to rest and read while I'm at the villa and enjoy 'living' in one place, as if I am a citizen." She smiled, imagining herself as a real citizen.

"Aaaaah," Marco said nodding, giving some thought to the idea of her staying in the country and not the city. "You get bored, no?"

"No. Why would you think I'd be bored?"

"Country very quiet...nothing doing."

She laughed, "Just staying in Tuscany will be exciting for me. I want to savour every moment of it. I also plan to visit Cortona and Florence. After I leave Tuscany, I will go to Venice for a few days before returning to Rome."

The following afternoon Marco escorted Francesca to Termini Station.

"I call, ok?" he said, "You call when you need something, ok?" and handed Francesca a mobile phone. She smiled and thanked him for everything and promised to call when she arrived at the villa.

As the train pulled away from the station, Francesca watched Marco fade into the distance and suddenly felt lonely. She shook herself, *'Come on girl. Now don't go getting soft— you're an independent woman: a gusty girl, remember?'* she told herself and then smiled, *'That's right. I'm a gutsy girl! I raised Aaron and Michelle on my own after Max deserted us, so I can do this. I can travel alone in a foreign country.'* She shrugged off the feeling and focused on the countryside flashing past.

24

In Segal Bay, Julia and Ben were snuggled together on the lounge in front of the television. O'Malley was draped across Julia's lap. While Ben dozed, Julia's thoughts drifted to the baby, loving the idea of becoming a mother. She gently laid her hand on her stomach and made a pledge to her unborn child, *'I'll be here for you, every step of the way, my darling. You'll be so loved. Your childhood will be wonderful, unlike my own lonely childhood.'*

Julia's parents were like strangers, popping in at odd times of her life, in between the hiring and firing of one indifferent nanny after the other until she was old enough to be packed off to boarding school. Remorseful tears filled her eyes as she struggled to recall when she had last spoken to either her mother or father, *'five or is it six years perhaps? The business demanded their attention, even keeping them from attending her wedding – huh, so Father said.'* Regret turned to anger. *'Why should I care anyway? They certainly don't. Not a word from them; money and power is all they care about. During a heated argument, Mother told me I was a mistake that I wasn't wanted, but they'd provided for me regardless, because it was their duty.'* Even with that knowledge, Julia still genuinely wanted to share the news of her baby with them, naively hoping a grandchild might reverse the situation.

The following morning Julia phoned her parents' Melbourne home. The housekeeper answered.

"Oh, Mrs Alderson is in Clayton Nursing Home and Mr Alderson is currently in Europe. He resides there six months of the year." She said in an official matter-of-fact manner, going on to tell Julia that her mother was suffering from some sort of a mental illness. "Dementia, I think Mr Alderson said it was."

"Excuse me?" Julia said stunned. "Will you repeat that please?"

"Of course, Mrs …"

As the housekeeper was speaking, Julia stumbled to a chair. When the call ended she hung her head and wept until she could cry no more, then dried her eyes and called Ben, but the sound of his voice set her off again.

Several hours later, they were in Melbourne and turning into the nursing home's driveway. Julia hesitated when getting out of the car. "Ben, I'm scared," she said, "I don't know what to expect, Mum has never liked me."

"Darling, I'll be with you." he said, gently wrapping a protective arm around her. "It'll be ok. Come on."

The nurse led Julia and Ben to Margaret's room; she knocked softly on the door before peeking inside. "She's awake," the nurse whispered, stepping aside for them to enter. Julia hesitated and looked at Ben, although her eyes were full of uncertainty, he gently coaxed her forward. Over by the bay window was a huge leather recliner. The nurse pointed to it. "Margaret's over there."

Julia gingerly moved closer. Her hand suddenly shot to her mouth to stifle her surprise at the sight of her thin and frail mother dwarfed by the size of the chair she was sitting in. She crouched down beside the recliner.

"How are you, Mum?" Julia asked, as she leaned over to kiss her on the cheek, but pulled back when Margaret turned and stared at her, with fear in her eyes and said, "Do I know you?"

Julia gasped as if she had been slapped. "I'm Julia," she whispered, suppressing her tears.

"Oh," Margaret said, confused.

"It's alright, Mum." Julia responded, patting Margaret's arm. "I'm just a friend. Would you like me to come and see you again?"

Margaret's eyes lit up and she smiled warmly at Julia, catching her totally off guard; never before had her mother smiled at her that way – ever!

After they left Clayton House, Julia and Ben sat in their car in silence, trying to digest what had just happened. Julia was slumped in her seat, lost for words, fighting back tears. She eventually looked at Ben and said, "I don't know which is worse, my mother's criticism of me or that she doesn't recognise me. I'd braced myself for the worst, but not for this. "She doesn't know me!"

A trail of tears as large as raindrops, spilled down Julia's pale cheeks and onto her jacket. She scrambled around in her bag looking for tissues and released a heavy sigh when she found them. Anger suddenly rose within her and exploded – ripping open the pack and pulling out tissues one after the other. "What happened to that strong, feisty, fashionable, business woman? What happened to her? Diminished to a small, fragile woman who doesn't know her own child. I never want our child to feel what I'm feeling at this moment – never, never!" Julia sobbed.

Ben was totally helpless to say or to do anything, other than to cradle Julia in his arms. He would never be so arrogant to tell her that he knows how she feels. He had no idea how she felt. All his life, he has only known parental love, never rejection. Julia came to realise that although her mother was lost in another world, and did not recognise her, the woman who replaced her mother was just a frail, gentle old lady, whom she could so easily forgive.

Before they left, the nursing staff told Julia that her father was taking care of Margaret, even though he had divorced her, remarried and relocated to Europe with his new family. She was not particularly perturbed by what her father did or did not do. He was no longer her family, Ben and Olivia were. As Julia was about to be a mother herself, she wanted to be the kind of mother to her child that she would have wished her own mother to have been to her; Olivia was her role model. Julia also realised that although her parents rejected her, she was not worthless; she was very worthwhile! Love, hate and prejudice are learned behaviours; forgiveness is a choice.

When they returned to Segal Bay, Julia told Ben that she wanted to see his mother. He gave her a quizzed look, "Are you sure you're up to it, baby? It's been a full-on couple of days, maybe you should get some sleep first, and see her in the morning, it's late."

"I'm ok, honey," she smiled, pleading with her eyes, "I must speak to mum, there's something important I have to tell her."

Olivia was just about to turn off the lights and go to bed, when she heard car doors slam. She flicked on the porch light and was startled when she opened the door.

"Ben! Julia! Is anything wrong? How is Margaret, sweetheart?"

"Mum, Mum, nothing is wrong. Jules just wanted to see you, that's all."

"Well don't just stand there, come inside."

"I'm sorry to disturb you this late, Mum, but, I…I need to say something – it's important." Julia was saying, as Olivia motioned them to sit down.

"What is it, sweetheart?"

"I want to apologise for being so horrid to you when we first met." Olivia glanced at Ben and he shrugged as Julia continued. "I had no idea what a mother's love was all about until I met you. I'm so grateful to you for teaching me. There was never a real connection between my mother and me. I don't know why there wasn't, it's just the way it was! I want you to know that I'm grateful for the wonderful and loving connection I have with you. I've never been able to say this to my mother, but I can say this to you – I love you, Mum. I feel privileged that you're my mother-in-law, my role model and my dearest friend."

Olivia hugged Julia, saying, "I too, am very privileged to have you for a daughter. I love you."

Olivia sat back and looked at Julia a moment and smiled, and then asked with a little trepidation, "How's your mother, darling?"

"Not good. She didn't know me." Olivia looked shocked. "But that's ok." Julia said quickly, to reassure her. "The woman I saw in the nursing home was too fragile to dislike. I've forgiven her and the past," Julia paused and smiled when Olivia sighed gently with relief. "You know, Mum, I actually feel free in my spirit. Forgiveness is so powerful."

Olivia touched Julia's cheek. "You look especially beautiful tonight, sweetheart."

"Mum, I'm happy, totally happy. No more dark clouds hanging over my head."

"Are you planning to see Margaret again?"

Julia glanced at Ben and he smiled at her. "I don't think so. I've made peace with her. She doesn't know me, it's too confusing for her and she's in good hands. I think it's best that I don't go back."

Julia had never looked more beautiful to Ben than she did at that moment. He was not thinking about her physical beauty, the kind the naked eye can see that fades with time, but her inner beauty, beauty that went to the core of her soul; the essence of her spirit. He, too, felt privileged, privileged that she was his wife and would soon be the mother of his child.

25

Olivia was surprised to hear Doris Day's voice coming from the jukebox when she came to the café that morning, and even more surprised to hear Ali in the kitchen, singing. Olivia stood by the door listening. "She is in love! Really in love, I would say. A secret love – hmmm, well we all know who that is."

Ali swayed as gracefully as a ballerina to the rhythm of the music, coming into the dining room humming, oblivious to her surroundings, carrying a tray loaded with crockery. She stopped dead in her tracks, almost toppling the lot when she saw Olivia.

"Olivia!" Ali barked, steadying herself. "I didn't hear you come in."

"Sorry, love, I didn't mean to startle you. What a lovely voice you have. I had no idea you could sing like that."

Ali blushed. "I haven't felt like singing before."

"It would seem that Pasquale is very special."

Ali glanced at Olivia and quickly shied away, responding with a shrug.

"Good morning, you two," Julia beamed.

"Hello, darling, you just missed hearing an angel sing."

Julia's brow crinkled, "What are you talking about, Mum?"

"Ali, she has a lovely voice."

Embarrassed, Ali dashed out to the dining room saying, "Hi Jules, can't chat, I've got heaps to do before we open."

Julia was bewildered. "What's going on?"

Olivia smiled and whispered, "Ali's in love…really in love."

"Ooh, I see." Julia grinned, leaning backwards far enough to observe Ali setting tables. "Come to think of it, she does have that look about her and she's mentioned family and children more than once during our breaks. I bet she'd be a wonderful mother. I really like Ali. Perhaps Ben and I should consider her for Godmother."

"Oh, love, that would be wonderful!"

"Yes, I think it will be for all of us. But to change the subject, Mum, how's Francesca?"

"She sounds fine. I had an email from her a few days ago. She's in Tuscany, staying at a B&B, Casa Bella something."

"Casa Bellavista?"

"That's it. The villa sounds lovely. Francesca said it's very peaceful, but very cold at the moment. It was ten degrees the day she arrived." Olivia shivered. "She also said her room is lovely and cosy and is furnished in eighteenth century pieces. She's staying in the Camera dei Fagiani. It's part of the main house and has wonderful countryside views; it even has a view from the loo." They both laughed, and Olivia continued, "Everyone's free to use the study, family and sitting room, which has a huge fireplace. Apparently they also have an impressive library. It sounds like Francesca might not come back. She loves the traditional farmhouse cuisine. She was full of information about the place, so much so that she sounds like a travel guide."

"I wouldn't blame her if she stayed, Mum. We could all do with some of that. When do we leave?"

Olivia laughed, "Right now, if it were possible, but I've a business to run.

Come on, love – we'll have to save that dream for another day."

"I'm right behind you, Mum." Julia said, following Olivia into the dining room.

****

Francesca shivered while waiting on Terontola Station for the train to Florence. The sun struggled to break through heavy cloud cover as icy winds penetrated the many layers of her light clothing. She could not recall ever feeling so cold, not even on the coldest winter day in Brisbane. Her loathing of cold weather did not foil her excitement of actually seeing *Michelangelo's' David*; if anything, it had warmed her spirit. For that reason alone, she ventured out into the chilly Tuscan autumn morning.

The station was deserted when she arrived, but as the minutes passed, dozens of other passengers appeared moments before the train pulled into the station; warm compartments and comfortable seats made the two hour journey a pleasant one. Upon arriving in Florence, Francesca consulted the city map she had with her one more time before leaving the station, getting her bearings to the Academy Museum, where the *David* was on display, well and truly fixed in her mind.

Dawdling along the way, she took in the sights, thinking how similar Florence was to Rome, narrow porfido filled streets, huge buildings, cathedrals, sidewalk cafés and thousands of tourists. The street market stalls she came across were fascinating and colourful, abundantly laden with beautiful leather and cashmere garments, gloves and other wondrous items, but shopping was not on her agenda, the *David* was.

The map Francesca had was easy to follow and she went directly to the Academy Museum where, outside, a line was already forming. As Francesca stood in line with other tourists, she could not help overhearing an American woman and an Australian man discussing the American elections. Obama was the favourite.

"If I have to," the woman said adamantly, in a broad twang. "I'll personally drive around and collect my family and friends and take them to the poll booths. Obama has to win!"

"Well," the Australian replied, "he'd better be good at his job, because whatever happens in your country seriously affects us in Australia. We're sick of Bush. What a dickhead!! Every time he opens his trap, he jams both feet in it. You Yanks must cringe whenever he's doing the official thing, like press conferences and such."

The woman laughed, "Oh yeah, we sure do."

"Our last PM was good to start with, and then he went off the rails and started climbing up Bush's arse. We eventually got rid him, but I'm still not sure about our new PM. Only time will tell about this one ..."

Before the woman could respond, the museum doors opened, ending the conversation as everyone shuffled inside. Security was tight at the entrance, everything was checked and rechecked, 'no photographs allowed' signs were boldly displayed everywhere; the flash is supposed to cause damage to the art works. *'Good way to boost postcards sales,'* Francesca mused, disappointed at the prohibited use of her camera.

Francesca casually shuffled along with the crowd, wandering around in large rooms, perusing art and marble statues she had seen in art and history books. As she was leaving one room, she came across the Australian. Francesca excused herself and asked if he knew where she could find the *David*.

"Oh hi, you're an Aussie?" he beamed.

Francesca returned his smile, nodding.

"I'm looking for it, too. Come on," he said, pointing straight ahead, "I think it's in the room up there…where in Aussieland are you from?"

"Segal Bay," she replied, looking around as they entered the hall, "Up north. Oh my goodness, there it is. It's magnificent! Wow!" she gasped in a breath.

They both stood still and gawked at the huge white form ahead of them. They then proceeded to move forward together, slowly, oblivious to everything else around them. They walked its circumference, carefully inspecting every inch. Francesca whispered to the Australian, "I'd read the *David* was huge, seventeen feet, but it seems so much larger here."

"Is that right, seventeen feet?"

"And did you know that Michelangelo wasn't the original artist of the sculpture?"

He nodded, "Hmm, I recall reading something about that."

As they circled the life-like statue a second time, Francesca said, "I read that Donatello and his assistant, Agostino di Duccio, created the first two sculptures. Agostino di Duccio shaped the legs, feet and started some of the drapery work prior to leaving the project; they say he left due to Donatello's death. Antonio Rossellino was hired and then eventually fired. I've no idea why he was fired, but Michelangelo was hired in 1501 about 25 years later, I think."

"Yep, that sounds about right." The Australian replied, totally in awe of the wondrous sight before him.

"Do you know why the upper body is larger than the lower part? ... and look at the hands – they're out of proportion with the body too. What do you make of that?"

The Australian shrugged, "I'm not sure."

Francesca thought a moment, and then said, "Could the size of the hands be some kind of metaphor about power and strength in throwing the stone and killing Goliath? – good versus evil?"

"I'm not sure, it could be." He shrugged, glancing at her, and then turning back to the sculpture, happy with her analysis. Francesca fixed her eye on the statue, amazed at how bloodless it seemed, yet so alive; the veins were tensed, as if ready for action. The lean, perfect torso and strong muscular shoulders made her think of Jake. She felt deeply remorseful for sending him away; her heart ached for the only man she wanted to be with. Thinking about Jake made her feel sad, so Francesca said goodbye to the Australian and left the museum.

She thought browsing through the market street stalls would be a delightful distraction, but she was wrong. Jake's image was alive in her thoughts, she saw him everywhere she looked; his voice echoed in her head. Francesca's heartache was relentless; she felt desperately lonely and wanted to go home.

The mobile Marco gave her before leaving Rome was ringing. The forgotten phone, when fished out of the shoulder bag, showed several missed calls.

"Buona sera, Francesca," Marco said, and she glanced at her watch, surprised to discover it was already late afternoon.

"Buona sera, Marco, it's good to hear from you," she replied, genuinely pleased to hear from him.

"I call many times – you good? No bored?"

She laughed. "No, I'm not bored?" then paused, "just a little homesick." There was silence, "Marco? Are you there?"

"Si, si, I here, when you go to Venice?"

"The day after tomorrow, why?"

"I thinking I meeting you and showing you to Venice."

"Really? That would be wonderful, Marco. Are you sure you can spare more time away from the office?"

"Si, si. I tell you in begin, work always here. It ok. I meet you at Venice – at station. What time train arrive?"

"1pm." She replied, feeling brighter. "I'll look forward to another of your wonderful tours, Marco. Thank you so much. I really do appreciate your kindness and generosity."

She could feel him smiling, "Ciao Francesca, we later talk."

With the idea of visiting Venice went the yearning to return home. 'A tour around Venice, how wonderful,' she thought, as a rebel smile creased her attractive features. 'How wonderful! Marco is wonderful! He's made such a difference to my holiday. I'm sure it wouldn't have been as exciting as this on my own. Hmmm, I like the idea of having a handsome Italian escort. Its' romantic – well, sort of, I can pretend,' she pondered, with an air of pleasure.

Francesca's visit to Cortona revealed another disappointment, only a slight one this time. The discovery was made when she went looking for the fountain seen in the movie, *Under the Tuscan Sun* and was told that the fountain was a movie prop and not a structure of the town. *'Of course it was,'* Francesca smiled to herself as she wandered past a narrow shop displaying cashmere jumpers and cardigans in the window. Without any hesitation, she went and purchased two very expensive jumpers to lift her spirits; and it worked.

After one last leisurely day at Casa Bellavista, Francesca caught the early morning train to Venice. She arrived in Tuscany as autumn began to take up residence. Through the window, as the train sailed along, she saw in the distance, a farmer on his tractor travelling up-hill, hard at work ploughing his green fields; the green slowly disappeared into the earth and became bare and brown. She found amusement in the scene; the farmer and his machine seemed so small, much like an insect climbing a wall. She smiled and continued to watch the country whizz by for a moment longer, then she settled back into her seat for the four hour journey, and began reading a novel. Prior to Francesca leaving Tuscany, Marco called to confirm their arrangements and mentioned that he had taken the liberty of booking rooms for her and himself, at *Locanda Ca Zose* on Giudecca Island.

26

Ali glanced up at the wall clock and cursed under her breath when Olivia said, "Shouldn't you be at the restaurant, Ali?" and immediately stopped what she was doing and made a dash for the door.

"Have to go, Olivia!" Ali yelled on her way out, and sprinted down the street, too distracted to notice she was being followed.

Gino was standing outside the restaurant, smoking the last of his cigarette when Ali arrived.

"G'day, Gino!" she chirped, passing him on her way in.

"Ciao, Bella!" he replied, stubbing out the cigarette before he tossed the butt in the sidewalk trash can. As he turned to go inside, a flash across the street caught his attention out the corner of his eye. He turned around just in time to see the hairdressers scurrying away, like thieves in the night. Gino had no time for those two, since he had heard the rumours they were spreading about Olivia and Ali. They had been trying stir up trouble for them for months. Gino thought of Olivia and Ali as family, and no one messes with his family. Reaching in his back pocket, Gino pulled out his mobile and dialled a number. "I need a cleaner," he casually said, and hung up.

Ali was breathless from running when she entered the kitchen. Pasquale looked at her. His face was taut and colourless as he furiously chopped onions, "You late again, Cara!"

Ali ignored the comment and said, "Hi guys, how's it going?" in her usual cheerful way as she dashed around the kitchen, getting her gear together.

There were a few mumbled replies, but a stern glance from Pasquale and the place went deadly quiet. Ali looked around the room and her smooth brow creased, "What's up? Why so quiet?"

The kitchen staff looked uncomfortable.

"Ok" she said, getting annoyed, "What's going on?"

"Ali!" Pasquale shouted in his familiar tone of dominance. "Everybudy work, no joke, no play and wasting tame!"

"Oooh, Mr Scary Pants, big boss man," she teased, but Pasquale was not laughing. He was seething that she was late, and now she's making fun of him in front of the staff. Ali glanced sideways and gave him a questioning look, catching a glimpse of the anger reflected in his dark eyes, and decided to confront him about it later.

The moment Pasquale stepped out of the kitchen the casual kitchen-hand leaned over to Ali and whispered, "He's been a real bastard, lately. Better be careful, he could get fist-happy, if you know what I mean."

Ali did not respond, but she had noticed the pleasure of working in the restaurant's kitchen had increasingly felt like work, very hard work. She missed the light-hearted bantering between her workmates and herself. As Ali thought about what she should do about the situation, the sound of screeching sirens outside sent a sudden chill through the kitchen. Everyone downed utensils and scurried outside to the street to see what the commotion was. Holiday-makers, day-trippers and locals of all ages, smelling of fruity sunscreen, had already gathered together like a swarm of locusts descending upon a farmer's crops. Those few without hats stood with hands up to their foreheads, shielding their faces from the glare of the hot early morning sun, watching smoke and flames billowing from the top floor of *Hudson House*, where *Cut & Dry* Salon was. The crowd cheered the fire brigade as soon as the situation was under control. Although the building was relatively unscathed, the contents of the salon were totally destroyed.

Jonathan and Harry came running up the street, pushing their way through the crowd. They were flushed and sweaty from the heat. They stood dead-still, too dumfounded to speak as they gawked at the carnage.

A hulk look-alike ambled up beside them. He folded his tree-trunk arms and fixed his sunken, dark eyes on the building and, without provocation, he said, in a deep penetrating baritone, "Looks like you two are leaving town."

"No, we're not!" Jonathan said, thawing in defiance.

"Yeah, you are. This," the hulk-man said, inclining his head towards the fire, "will put you out of business."

"Oh no," Jonathan responded, puffed up with arrogance, "We're insured."

Harry shook his head, "No, no we're not. Business hasn't been good lately, I had to delay the insurance payments."

Jonathan turned slowly. His jaw set firm. "What?" He yelled in his highest pitch as the crowd was dispersing. Many stopped suddenly when they heard the noise and turned back to witness Jonathan raise his fist, about to punch Harry full-force in the face and, the hulk-man catching the swing mid-air, sent Jonathan stumbling backwards, arms flapping in a circular motion, trying miserably to steady himself, and landing flat out on his back. A roar of laughter cut through the air.

The mammoth stranger remained where he stood. Without moving a muscle, he boomed across to Harry, "You'd better grow balls before this prick murders you."

Harry shook himself sensible, realising the truth in that statement and arched up. He stormed over to where Jonathan lay sprawled out on the footpath. Jonathan held out his hand for Harry to help him up.

"This is your fault!" Harry screamed, slapping the hand out of the way as he unleashed years of frustration, "Your fault! If, if you hadn't have lied all those years ago all this, this wouldn't be happening, and you wouldn't be holding me to ransom – Harry do this, Harry get that, like I'm some fucking slave. I hate you! I hate you! I wanted to tell the truth, but you wouldn't let me. Damn you! I stole the money from Elizabeth to get away from YOU!" He screamed an eye-bulging, vein-popping scream.

The world suddenly seemed still and very silent. Harry looked around. The blood drained from his stunned features as his lips quivered; hundreds of eyes were staring at him; everyone was listening.

"I put the money back," he said, hoping to redeem himself, and began to explain what had happened. "Jonathan and I worked at the same salon – in Melbourne. We'd just started dating, but I wanted out. I was too afraid to tell him because he is a CONTROL FREAK!! Elizabeth Swanson, Ali's mother …" murmuring rippled through the crowd when Ali's name was mentioned. "Yeah, Ali," Harry admitted, "who works at the Corner Café. Her mother was the client I stole the money from. She discovered the money was gone when she paid her bill," said Harry in tears, getting distraught. "She always paid by credit card, but she didn't that day! I wanted to fess up, but Jonathan made me slip the money in her coat pocket. He tried to convince Elizabeth that she was mistaken, but she knew I took the money and confronted me. But I repeatedly denied any wrong-doing. We," Harry shrugged, "we were fired anyway and had to leave the state. He," Harry snarled, pointing an accusing finger at Jonathan, "wanted revenge and sent horrible and threatening anonymous emails to Elizabeth, at intervals over the years. He was obsessed with wanting her to pay for us getting fired. He believed his own lie, and then Ali arrived in town."

"Yes?" Ali asked, stepping out of the crowd.

Harry gasped. "Oh, I am so, so sorry, Ali."

"Where do I fit in to all of this?"

"Jonathan–oh I'm not sure what he was planning, Ali. But if he couldn't punish Elizabeth, he would've punished you."

"He's lying, Ali. It was his idea. He stole the money from your mother."

"Shut up, you creep! You befriended me hoping to *hurt* my mother." Ali lowered her voice and crouched down, saying, "You're so lucky that I'm a different person, otherwise – well, otherwise, that's all. You're abhorrent!" She spat before hurrying away to call her mother.

Jonathan managed to scramble to his feet and was about to stagger away.

"Where're you going?" boomed the hulk-man.

"Home," Jonathan bleeped.

"No point, there's nothing there."

A pitiful animal cry came from the pit of Jonathan's belly, running the two blocks to his house, as if the devil were chasing him. The huge man casually got into his vehicle and drove slowly to the hairdresser's home. Harry had already left. He had taken the four-wheel drive and headed south, out of town.

Jonathan turned into his street and staggered up to where his home used to be, and fell in a heap, sobbing. His art treasures and designer furnishings were all destroyed. His home was incinerated. There was nothing salvageable in the pile of damp, black cinders. Everything the hairdressers owned was obliterated in both fires.

The ominous man arrived on the scene about the same time as Jonathan. He got out of his vehicle and walked over to where Jonathan laid, casting a dark shadow over him. Devoid of any empathy, he looked down at the miserable, sobbing mess at his feet. "Everything has a use-by date, especially pricks like you."

Jonathan sat up and spat at him.

The man's deep-set eyes turned black and cold, "Oh," he said, shaking his head, "you shouldn't have done that."

27

It was an overcast afternoon, with a chill in the air when Francesca arrived at Venezia, Santa Lucia Train Station on the west side of Venice. Marco was there, waiting as promised. He greeted Francesca warmly and took her bag in one hand while he carried his in the other.

"Come," he said, "we go," then marched off in the direction of the vaporetti.

Francesca was tired from the long journey, and struggled to keep a steady pace with Marco. With his hands occupied with luggage, Marco inclined his head to things of interest. *'If his hands were free, they would be chopping the air as well'*, Francesca reasoned, observing Marco from behind with some amusement, *'Who said Italians couldn't talk if their hands were full?'* Her bag did little summersaults every time he uttered a word.

When Francesca had not replied to anything he had said, Marco stopped and turned around to discover that she was hurrying to catch up.

"What wrong, Francesca?" He asked, "Why you run? There no rush," he snapped, rolling the r, and his eyes as he jerked his head backwards, clicking his tongue, as he did the first day they met.

"I'm running to keep up with you, Marco. You're walking so fast."

Marco's brow creased, momentarily puzzled, and then it smoothed out and travelled upwards, "Aaaah, I rushing?" He said, finally understanding.

Francesca nodded, "Like a man on a mission," she sighed heavily.

"What this mission man?"

Francesca shook her head and made a sound that resembled a laugh,

"Nothing, Marco. Never mind, it's all good."

"Ok, you good now?" He asked, satisfied that they were both now in sync.

When they reached Roma Square, Marco gently placed a protective hand on the small of Francesca's back and guided her onto the vaporetti and to a vacant window seat. He turned to Francesca, about to say something, and stopped. The expression on her face and the delight in her eyes; she was positively glowing. Marco sat back and left Francesca to enjoy the journey.

Everything seemed surreal to her. The sounds from diverse groups of tourists and locals babbling in their foreign languages vibrated throughout the vessel, marvellously blending in with the rhythm of the engine and sound of rushing water the vaporetti made as it snaked its way around Canal Grande; the odd sounds seemed like an awkward symphony to her. *'I'm actually in Venice!'* She thought, with a sense of disbelief, and a quiver of excitement ran through her. While travelling past old, majestic architecture, standing proud and imperfect, in her mind Francesca could hear Luciano Pavarotti singing *Nessum Dorma*. She imagined his voice echoing though the buildings and down the canal.

Marco explained that the canal was the residents' only means of getting from place to place.

"Even when moving house?" She asked.

"Si, for everything, look," he said, pointing to a passing craft full to the brim with furniture. She was silent a moment, trying to imagine herself moving all her possessions from one house to another that way, then doused the thought and shuddered, giving Marco a horrified look.

"The expense would be enormous."

"Oh, si expensive, but it this way in my city."

"Why did your countrymen build their city on a lagoon?"

"To escape barbarian invasions, after fall of Roman Empire, first people come about fifth or maybe sixth centuries. The people come from mainland Venice, they fighting very hard, working very hard to making Venice most unique city in world. First they build rafts supporting by strong wooden poles. They connect raft together, build house on them, making wooden pathways. When Venice have many, many citizens they give city title. Venice is trading city making business with many countries; but what making Venice more famous, in year 828, two Venetian merchant stealing Apostle Mark body from Alesssandra in Egypt and bringing to Venice. Now he Patron Saint of Venice – Basilica of San Marco."

The vaporetti pulled in at Accademia, just as Marco finished the history lesson. They disembarked and walked a short distance through a maze of intriguing narrow calles. On their way to the hotel, Francesca could not resist gazing enviously into a few shop windows of famous designers, Gucci, Chanel and Prada. "My friends would go crazy shopping here," Francesca said, peering in Chanel's window.

"What about you, Francesca? You like boo-ti-ful garment?"

"Oh yes, Chanel's one of my favourite designers and I adore Chanel 5 … but my lifestyle doesn't cater for such extravagance, neither does my bank account," she laughed. "I'm happy to settle for smart casual and an occasional bottle of Chanel 5, when I can afford it."

"Your husband not provide well for you?"

Marco's comment surprised Francesca, "My *husband*?"

"Si."

She laughed sarcastically. "My husband abandoned his son and his daughter and me years ago. I am," she paused, "was the provider, Marco, and I provided well for my family and for myself," she said a little too sharply, irritated by the memory. "Oh, I didn't mean to sound so callous, Marco," Francesca said when he stared at her. "Please accept my apology."

"No, no, apology, Cara. I shock, your husband abandon you and bambinos. He crazy!"

She smiled awkwardly, "He's a gambler. After selling our home to pay his debts, I started all over again with my children. He's gone and that's a blessing. It's in the past. I don't want to talk about it."

"As you wish," he nodded. "May I speak about children? What is age?"

"Certainly," Francesca beamed with pride, "Aaron is twenty and very independent. He has a part-time job and lives close to the university where he is studying forensic science. Michelle is nineteen. She's in Sydney doing a veterinarian nurse traineeship."

"You alone now?" Marco cut in.

Francesca looked surprised. "I hadn't thought of it as being alone. I do live on my own, yes, but I don't feel alone."

"You got special friend?"

The question caught Francesca completely off guard. The pain of recalling her mistake was silently suffocating her. Pretending to be distracted with something in the store window, Francesca turned away quickly as tears surfaced. She stood with her back to Marco, facing the window trying to regain her composure.

"Oh," she said, pulling out a tissue, dabbing her eyelids, "I've something in my eye. These contact lenses are so uncomfortable at times."

Marco nodded, totally aware of what had just happened, "Come, we go to hotel and later we eat."

Francesca smiled, thinking how often Marco would say, *'Come, we eat, as the remedy to a problem. If he keeps it up, I will be the size of a house.'*

Although food was the furthest thing from Francesca's mind, as a gesture of gratitude to Marco's kindness, she surrendered to the temptation of another delicious Italian meal.

"That sounds like a plan," Francesca grinned, "a wonderful plan, my friend. I'm starving."

Marco's brow creased, "Why not you say something? If you hungry, we eat now."

"I'd rather shower and change first."

"Ok," he shrugged, "we go now."

At the hotel, Marco suggested they meet in the lobby at 8pm. "This give plenty time for relaxing and be better to enjoying evening. Holiday for enjoying, not thinking of other things, si?"

She smiled warmly, about to hug him for being sensitive to her needs, but checked herself, mindful of not sending him the wrong message; instead she said, "Si," and he smiled.

While they sat in a café near Accademia Bridge, Marco's eyes were firmly fixed on Francesca, observing her with a keen interest. He thought she was beautiful, especially with the way she looked around at her surroundings with child-like excitement, unable to harness her delight at the difference in the city at night. There was excitement in her voice when she told him she thought the canal resembled a magical fairyland the way everything glowed, and how the lights from nearby buildings dancing on the canal had turned its murky waters into black shimmering velvet. He had never noticed it until she told him.

Francesca's eyes sparkled with excitement. "Now this," Francesca said, with a wave of her hand, "is the magic I was hoping to find at Trevi Fountain – the romance, the beauty, Venice has it. Venice is so beautiful Marco, it's a wonderland. I can easily imagine music in the wind, and in the rhythm of the waves – everywhere. Just look around you, it's not a fantasy, it's real," she smiled.

Marco looked at her with a wishful heart and said, "Venice romantic city, it easy to falling in love."

Francesca blushed and quickly picked up the menu. "It's my treat; you're my guest tonight, Marco." Before he could protest she said, "I'd be offended if you refused my hospitality. You've been so gracious, so kind, so wonderful to me. You must let me say thank you in this small way."

She watched him sit erect in the chair, as if wrestling with his pride and then relaxed, smiling warmly, "Ok," he shrugged, "if give you pleasure, Francesca."

"It does, Marco. Thank you."

After leaving the café, they bought gelato and walked arm-in-arm around the canal. Francesca casually said, "It's difficult to imagine the world in such turmoil, when surrounded by beauty and peaceful ambience."

He nodded, but he was deep in his own thoughts.

"It's a perfect night," she continued. "I never expected a warm evening breeze this time of year – everything is perfect." She paused thinking, *'well almost perfect.'*

Marco did not miss the pause or her expression change for a split second and then brighten up again. "Venice is magical. I love Venice! I'd like to come back some day, to Venice and to Tuscany. I could live in Tuscany."

Marco's eyes lit up "You want live in Tuscany?"

"If Tuscany was in Queensland, yes. I could never leave Australia and live elsewhere. Australia is the best place on earth. Other countries are wonderful to visit and to appreciate – but never to live. Well, perhaps only for a short time."

"Your country is intrigue. I visit, maybe? I go abroad to business. I can make business in Australia. I see Ben, too."

"That'd be wonderful, Marco! You could meet all of my friends and my dearest friend, Olivia, Ben's mother. I could show you around."

"Francesca, I go to my village tomorrow, you come meet my family?"

She stopped and faced him. "Oh, no, I can't, Marco. Thank you, but I want to go home. I must go back. I, I've decided to leave in the morning."

28

Just about everyone in town heard about Harry's confession, including Gino. When Ali asked for time off, he said, "Sure Bella, unhappy chefs make food taste bitter and that's not good for business," he teased. "Take a couple of days, if you need them."

Ali gave Gino a quick hug and ran up to the Corner Café. News of the incident was buzzing all over the place. Olivia looked up when Ali burst through the door. Maddie nodded to Olivia, indicating that she and Julia would look after things while she talked to Ali.

"Ali! Over here!" Olivia waved, and Ali followed her to the booth at the far end of the room.

"I guess it's time I told you the whole story," Ali said, catching her breath. She ended it by saying, "I still haven't told my parents where I am. They know I'm safe and they know what those creeps did and why." Ali shook her head in disgust. "My parents had no idea what the emails were about. Mum had totally forgotten about the theft, she was stressing about the emails, thinking I was in danger. She's so relieved to know who was behind them. She's ok now, though."

"Well, darling," Olivia said, "I really do think you should tell your parents where you are."

Ali shook her head. "I can't risk Rhys finding me, or hurting them as payback. He's dangerous, no matter what his family say about him finding *God*."

Olivia's brow creased with a questioning look.

"Huh! There was an article in a magazine about Rhys and how he found God while in prison, etc, etc. It's a lie! He's an actor – a very convincing actor, Olivia." Ali studied Olivia for a moment. "I'm curious, why do you keep insisting I should tell my parents where I am?"

"Oh, I guess I'm just getting old."

Ali screwed up her face. "What? C'mon, Olivia, there's something else going on here; fess up."

"I don't know why after all these years, but I keep thinking about my mother and what kind of life she's had and if she's happy."

"What are you talking about? You said your parents owned this café, you knew your mother."

Olivia's eyes looked momentarily sad when she told Ali that she was adopted.

"Oh, don't misunderstand me, I had a wonderful childhood and I loved my darling parents, as they me, but since their death I've wondered about my birth-mother."

"Were you angry when your parents told you?"

"Oh, no, not at all! My parents had a little information about her situation. She was twenty years old and unmarried. Her family insisted she put me up for adoption to save a scandal. I'm sure she made a huge sacrifice to give me a better chance in life; for that I'm so grateful. But still, I do wonder about her." Olivia cupped Ali's hands in hers and looked into her eyes, pleading. "I'd be out of my mind with worry if Ben vanished from my life the way you have from your parents' life, Ali. Tell them!"

Ali shook her head, "I can't risk it, Olivia."

Sarah Connelly, a resident of Manor Village and a frequent visitor to the café, was sitting in the booth behind Ali and Olivia, listening to their conversation. Her well-worn features creased into tiny lines of sadness, recounting her destiny, written before she arrived on this earth.

Even decades after, Sarah could clearly hear the harshness in her parents' voices, *'Will Alistair is not of our social standing, Sarah, he's Aboriginal'*, they protested often. Will was a stolen-generation child, adopted into a kind and loving family. His charm and good looks won over just about everyone who crossed his path. Sarah saw him as her knight in shining armour. She adored Will, as he did her. He was intelligent, funny and had great ambitions of designing innovating and provocative furniture, unlike anything she had ever seen. He promised Sarah the best life possible. His electrifying energy evoked in Sarah an indelible passion for life that would sustain her for the future.

All their plans and dreams disintegrated the night Sarah answered a knock at the door and found two woeful policemen standing there. She trembled in disbelief. One spoke, but she didn't hear a word he said; his mouth moved silently as he handed her a small, blue velvet box and a card they found in Will's coat pocket with the name *Sarah* written on the envelope in Will's bold, flamboyant style. A muffled, "I'm so sorry, Miss Connelly," echoed in her head, seconds before everything went black. Will was killed on his way to collect her; it was to be their wedding night. When Sarah discovered she was pregnant, she wanted desperately to keep her child,

Will's child, but her parents had other plans. Sarah was drugged and tricked into signing the adoption papers and the baby was silently whisked away, *to a good home*, she was told.

As Olivia stood up, about to go back to the kitchen, she said, "Well, at least think about it, love," and turned around, "Oh, Sarah, hello, darling, I didn't see you there. How are you?' Olivia asked, and sat down opposite her.

"Ali, wait a minute, love," she said, and then turned back to Sarah, "Have you had tea yet?"

"Not yet, love."

"Good, then you can join me. Your usual?"

When Sarah nodded, Ali said, "I've got it."

"Oh, Olivia, you're a darling girl."

"Hardly a girl," she laughed.

Sarah patted Olivia's hand and smiled, 'Compared to me, darling, you are. You're such a joy to all of us, my dear. Tom loved coming here. He loved Ali and you, all of you." Sarah leaned forward and whispered, "Tom and I would often have long chats. The other women at the Manor were after him, poor soul. They wouldn't leave him be, until he gave them what for," she grinned mischievously, "but he knew he was safe with me. We're lucky to have you here, Olivia. Tom said it rightly when he said you serve everything with a cup of love."

Olivia's eyes glistened, and she gently squeezed Sarah's frail, knobbly hand.

"I think of you, darling, and the others as my family."

"I overheard you talking to Ali, about being adopted," Sarah said, looking a little sheepish, "I didn't mean to eavesdrop."

Olivia smiled, and Sarah continued, "I believe your mother wanted to keep you, but fate stepped in and took you in another direction – to here. You were born out of love, raised with love, and now you share that love with all of us. Olivia, I do believe that was your destiny. Our paths are predestined before we're born, sweetheart. But, many never discover their purpose; they just rattle around this big planet, full of self-pity, because their plans failed, instead of making new ones."

Olivia listened, thinking what Sarah was saying made sense. "And," Sarah said, "I also believe your mother is living a good life and carries you in her heart. She wouldn't want you worrying about her. She would want you to be happy. Now," the old woman said, smiling, when Ali arrived with their tea, "let's enjoy this before it goes cold!"

29

The taxi pulled up in front of Francesca's home a few minutes before midnight.

'Home, what a wonderful sight,' she thought, encapsulated by a warm sentimental feeling. She arrived home earlier than expected without telling anyone, planning to make use of the extra days to rest and to clear her mind; she was emotionally and physically spent. Jake was still haunting her thoughts. For a brief moment she thought she saw his silhouette on the veranda, but dismissed it.

Francesca sighed heavily and looked down at her luggage as if it were another unwanted burden, and then bent her travel-weary frame to retrieve it. Jake stepped out of the shadows and said, "I'll take that my darling."

Francesca shook herself, thinking she had imagined she had heard Jake's voice; the voice that had been rattling around in her head all the way home, and then sprung to life when he embraced her. They clung to each other with such urgency, afraid the other might disappear if either let go.

"You're real, you are real," she whispered, studying every detail of his handsome face as she tenderly kissed him.

"How did you know I wanted so desperately to see you, to touch you, to look at you?"

Jake could not explain why he was there at that moment. He just felt he had to go to Francesca's house. He sat on the porch and waited for what, he had no idea until that moment. "Someone or something wants us to be together, baby, because I had this *feeling* to come here. That's the only way I can explain it."

The next couple of days were everything a woman, *enamoured*, could imagine. Jake had awakened in her the spirit of her youth, driven by euphoric passion. But Francesca still savagely wrestled with the idea that their relationship would rob Jake of the family she knew he wanted. *'Love is a strong emotion, it can be so selfish'*, she reasoned, *'it can also be unselfish.'*

"My childrearing days are over," she told him. Jake tried and failed miserably to convince her that having children no longer mattered to him. Her reply would always be the same. "You say that now in the heat of fervour, but a few years from now regret would creep in on our off days – and there'll be off days, darling. Marry someone younger and have your family."

She loved him with the essence of her spirit and for that reason alone she sent him away a second time; rather to do that than have him eventually resent her. Since there was no convincing Francesca she was overreacting he left, shattered.

When Francesca thought she was strong enough to brave the world, she phoned Olivia unprepared for her own reaction at the sound of her best friend's voice. Francesca broke down and confessed to Olivia what she regrettably had done, *again*.

"Francesca, Francesca, why do you have this problem about the age difference between you and Jake? It's only eight years. That's nothing these days. Jake loves you, woman. Why can't you grasp that? No, that man more than loves you, Francesca, he's besotted. I'm on his side."

"But, Olivia, he wants children, it's too late for me."

"Who said so?"

"I'm almost forty-five."

"So? You are fit and healthy and you look fabulous!"

"You're a wonderful liar my friend," she laughed, "thanks for trying to make me feel better."

"Francesca, I'm not in the habit of manufacturing flattery. Now call Jake and tell him to come back."

"It's too late, Olivia, he's gone. I don't know where to find him."

A welcome-home sign hanging above the café counter, along with friends and regular customers, awaited Francesca when she arrived to begin her shift. After the fanfare and revelry had settled down, the morning was taken up with Francesca giving account of her exciting trip. Many were surprised to learn she was unimpressed with Vatican City. Francesca's lovely features contorted in utter disgust. "The decadence was far too depressing," she said, looking around the room. "I'm terribly sorry if I offend anyone, but, in my opinion, there's nothing *holy* at the Vatican. I had to get out of there, quickly; the place was suffocating. That so-called holy place is full of opulence, while millions live in squalor and die of starvation. Now tell me what is holy about that? Vatican City's wealth and decadence opposes everything spiritual and humanitarian." Francesca's shoulders slumped, totally disillusioned. "After visiting the Vatican, I see Catholicism in the same way as other religions: politically motivated with an unquenchable lust for power, with little regard for human suffering. The artwork on the Vatican walls spoke more than a thousand words to me, most of which is so violent, that I cringed and had to turn away. I felt sick. Marble statues of one Caesar or another and various popes lined the halls, exhibiting a grand example of vanity and futuristic public relations. No one would have ever known them if they hadn't commissioned sculptures of themselves."

Kate broke in, "Religious beliefs only have value because people agree they do, for whatever reason. Religion in general is a prime example of that, and it also robs individuals of equality."

"How so?" Max Turner asked, while spooning two sugars into his coffee.

"Every religion claims superiority over the other. Where's the humanitarian equality in that?" Kate replied.

Max thought a minute, and then nodded, "Oh yeah, I see what you mean. Hmmm," he said, raising his brow. "I guess that's another way of looking at it. Yeah," he drawled, "I can see how the wealth would be an insult to human suffering; as my Italian mate would say, *'Insulto alla miseria.'*

Annie Jasper chipped in, "And what about pro-choice?" She asked and continued before anyone could reply. "The hierarchy and self-righteous do-gooders believe they can dictate to women, what's right and what's wrong." Annie paused. "Enter power-tripping, moral agitators on the rampage, willing to do anything: even murdering doctors and bombing abortion clinics to make their point. If these activists were really sincere, they would provide and care for the mothers during the pregnancy and then later help care and provide for the children." Annie said, catching everyone's eye for a split second and saw scepticism. "Well, why not? It would be a more logical solution to murdering doctors." Annie paused a moment, giving thought to whether she should tell her friends of her own experience and then, in one breath, she said, "I was once absolutely dead-set against abortion, until I was faced with the decision myself. I've had an abortion and I don't for one second regret it. It's as simple as that," she blurted out, as all eyes were upon her. "It was years ago," she continued, "before we came to Segal Bay. My first husband was really something. He abused our children, and me. When I discovered I was pregnant again, I knew I couldn't let him hurt another child. The hierarchy didn't know us or our circumstances and if they had, would any of them care? I very much doubt it. Annie took a breath and looked at the floor momentarily and then said, thoughtfully. "I've made many mistakes over my lifetime and I paid dearly for every one of them. The Bible says: *Judge not lest ye be judged*, and yet the strongest judgement comes from so-called Christians. Scanning the faces of those listening to her she said, "I'm not ashamed of what I did. I did what I had to do. I'd be happy to confront anyone of those hypocrites and remind them that their Jesus said, *He who is without sin, cast the first stone*. Annie laughed, "I guess that means I'm safe." and the others laughed as well, easing the awkwardness in the room.

"What was your most favourite place in Italy, Francesca?" Rose asked, to change the subject.

"It was all wonderful in so many different ways."

Olivia was standing by the kitchen door, listening to Anton as, well as listening to Francesca and the customers.

"… Francesca has to work it out for herself, darling, we can't interfere," he was saying.

"But."

"No buts!"

"But what, Mum?" Julia asked, walking up behind her.

Olivia spun around. "Hello, sweetie," she said, glancing sheepishly at Julia,

"Oh, don't mind me. I'm just talking to myself."

Julia casually draped an arm over Olivia's shoulders. Leaning in for a better view, "Have I missed anything?" she asked, scrutinising the scene in the dining room. "Wow, Francesca looks amazing! Something wonderful must have happened to her, she's glowing."

Anton smiled, and Olivia gave him a curious look. She was about to ask him why he was smiling, but remembered Julia. Her brows knitted together as she studied Francesca. Then suddenly, Olivia's hand shot to her mouth to stifle a gasp, and her head spun sideways to look at Anton for confirmation. He put a finger to his lips and nodded.

30

Several months later, the Corner Café was preparing to celebrate the arrival of Ben and Julia's child.

Julia was resting on the couch in a euphoric mood; grateful she had reconciled with her mother, grateful for Ben. "My darling Ben, what a wonderful man you are." She whispered, "You're my life." She hugged her round belly, "and so are you, my little Angelo."

She was smiling, sublimely happy, when a sudden sharp-piercing pain struck. Her hands shot up to her head. She gripped it tightly and let out an agonising scream. Anton was standing beside her, she saw him moments before losing consciousness. Anton alerted Olivia.

As soon as her son was delivered by caesarean section, Julia drew her last breath, and stood by her lifeless body, watching the scene. One moment everyone was rushing about, and the next, the theatre went deadly still. The baby's healthy cry, demanding attention, brought everyone back to animation.

The Corner Café was closed. Olivia, Ben and their closest friends were gathered together in the Segal Bay Hospital waiting room. Everyone feared the worst when the forlorn surgeon appeared in the doorway looking awkwardly uncomfortable, being the bearer of bad news. His sombre expression said it all. Ben glanced up and read his expression. He sprang to his feet and ran from the room; refusing commiseration or to let Julia go. He felt he would never be ready to let her go.

Ali watched Ben leave. Her heart was breaking for him. She knew she could not console him, but wanted desperately to see the baby, to hold him and to shield him from his father's grief and from the loss of his mother. Her thoughts turned to Julia. *'Poor dear, dear Julia. How very sad, you won't be able to hold your baby or see him grow up."* Anger welled up inside her, *"It's so unfair, damn it!'*

Julia was listening and watching her and whispered. *"It's ok Ali. I want you to look after Angelo and love him as your own. I trust you."*

Ali was restless and anxious. She went over to Olivia when the surgeon left and, in a low voice, said, "I want to see the baby. I want to see Angelo."

Olivia looked dazed. She turned to Ali. "Julia died from a blood clot. The headaches were serious – now she's dead." Olivia's eyes flashed as anger hardened her lovely face. "Anton didn't warn me," she whispered to Ali. "Not one word! He could have …!"

"Stop it, Olivia!" Ali shook her gently. "Just stop it! You know how it works. We have Angelo to think about now. Has everyone forgotten him? Ben can't take care of him yet. So it's up to us. I want to see him. Come on, Olivia," she said with authority, taking her gently by the arm. Julia smiled, *'Ali's perfect to care for Angelo, she will love and protect him.'* She followed Ali and Olivia to the nursery, while the others remained behind and quietly comforted each other.

Olivia walked like the living-dead along the corridor. She could not see or feel Anton's presence. Had he deserted her? Ali's concern for the baby's future slowly subsided as she came nearer to the nursery; the bond between her and the child strengthened with Julia's integration. Ali tapped lightly on the nursery window. The nurse stopped what she was doing and looked up. Ali then pointed to the second cot on the right, mouthing "Rossetti." The nurse waved, acknowledging the name, then carefully shuffled cots around and gently wheeled Angelo into view.

The moment Ali's eyes fell upon the child, Julia transferred her love for her son to Ali, like a lightning bolt smashing the earth during an electrical storm. The force was strong enough for Olivia to turn, just in time to see Julia standing beside Ali and the glow that surrounded them, and immediately understood what was happening.

"I have to find Ben." She told Ali, and left her standing at the nursery window.

In the car Olivia, peeved with herself, ranted in tears, "How could I've been so selfish, doubting him? But I guess I'm just human."

The ranting stopped when Olivia recalled the day Anton mentioned that Ben and Julia had their paths to follow and, so had she, but would not tell her anything else.

'Is this what he was referring to? Julia's death was their destiny?' Ali flashed into her mind, she was singing Secret Love. Olivia gasped. *'Oh, it's Ben, not Pasquale.'*

From the road Olivia saw Ben's charcoal Jaguar in the cemetery car park. She drove in and parked beside it. Before opening the door, she hesitated a brief moment, sighing deeply, wondering what she could say to console her son; words were pointless at a time like this. With a heavy heart she made her way along the pebble pathway that led to Anton's grave, and to where she knew her son would be.

Ben looked up briefly when Olivia sat down beside him. Neither spoke.

Ben stared at the ground while Olivia gazed about her and thought how beautiful the cemetery grounds were. An immaculate rich green lawn, sprawling up to garden beds, bursting with various species of vibrant blooms that flawlessly blended with an azure sky; birds merrily chirping in surrounding jacarandas made an exquisite tapestry vista, woven into a very sad day.

"You know, Mum," Ben finally said, breaking the silence, "this is the first time I've been here since Dad died." Olivia silently reached for her son's hand and gently squeezed it.

"It never felt like he was gone, that's why I never came here," he said, turning his sombre face towards his mother. "Did it feel like that for you, too?"

Olivia nodded, her eyes softening, recalling the joy she felt the first time she saw Anton after his passing. "He came back," she said. "He's been looking after us all this time. For many years I thought it was my imagination, but when Ali felt your father's presence too, I knew it wasn't."

"Will Jules come back too, Mum?" Tears welled up in his eyes and overflowed, spilling down his strong masculine face. Olivia took a tissue from her pocket and dabbed the tears away.

"I don't think so, darling. Julia has to move on, but you'll see her again. At least you know she's ok, and knowing that death isn't final should ease your pain."

"From my own experience with Dad, I can fathom what you're saying. But…"

Olivia looked perplexed, "What do you mean? Did you see your father?"

Ben looked embarrassed and shrugged. "If it wasn't for Dad, I'd probably be divorced now." Olivia frowned as Ben continued, "He was the one who alerted me to what Maria was doing. He visited me one night, I thought I was dreaming, to tell me to wake up to myself, and when I started to take notice of how Maria was playing me, I realised that Dad was real – well as real as a ghost can be," he half grinned.

They sat quietly together on the seat, locked in their own thoughts.

"You know, darling," Olivia said, coming to terms with the hopelessness of holding on to Anton. "As much as I love your father and so dearly want him with me, it's not the same as having him really with me. It isn't healthy to grieve to the point of excluding a physical loving relationship from your life. You're young, with a full life ahead of you in time, when you are ready. Julia wouldn't want you to reject love. Your life is now about Angelo."

Ben looked stunned. "What did you say?"

"Your life is now about *Angelo*."

No one knew the baby's name. How, who told you his name, Dad?"

"No, darling, Ali called him that. I just thought…well I don't know what I thought now that you mention it. I've no idea how she knew." Olivia said, trying to recall if Julia had told her, "Aaah," she said, remembering the scene at the hospital. "I expect Julia told her."

"What? When?"

"Ali and I were at the nursery. I was feeling sorry for myself and wasn't really paying attention, something made me look at Ali. That was when I saw Julia standing beside her, the glow around them was so brilliant; I sensed she was asking Ali to look after the baby. I pulled myself together and knew I had to find you."

Ben shook his head. "Mum, Mum," he pleaded, utterly helpless. "I don't know what to do! It's too much. I need to get away. Jules was my life and now she…she's gone." He choked, barely managing to get the words out. He fidgeted with the twig he was holding, then threw it aside and stood up. He ran his hands through his hair then covering his face, he fell to his knees sobbing. Nothing Olivia said would console him. So she sat quietly beside her son while he wept. Olivia looked out at the garden and from the periphery of her vision saw Anton standing under a jacaranda, and knew that he too would soon be leaving.

31

Julia's death was an enormous shock to everyone who knew the Rossetti family, especially the retirees at Manor Village. Most of them dined at the Corner Café at least two or three times a week; it was an integral part of their ritualistic lifestyles. Francesca knew the lifeless café would have a serious impact on the residents, and made preparation to open as usual. She also needed an excuse to keep busy.

That morning, she left home early with a heavy heart, and took a leisurely drive along the foreshore hoping to feel better. Gazing through the windscreen, Francesca could see the Bay was at peace with the world as the sun slowly rose in a crisp cerulean sky, preparing to blast the earth with its scorching rays. Foot traffic began filling the walkway. Ambling elderly couples holding hands, marching dog walkers, women struggling to shed their winter skin, young mothers pushing prams and a few middle-aged men and women denying their lost years, pounded the footpath with brute force, determined to push back time. Taking in the sights had only slightly lifted Francesca's mood. She gently caressed her stomach and gave thanks for the life she carried, asking only that her child be safe.

When she drove into the café car park, Nicky and Maree were waiting there for her. They waved, and rushed over to the car. "We thought you could use some help." Nicky smiled, showing a row of perfect teeth. Maree rubbed her hands together, trying to sound cheerful and asked, "Where do we start? Anything to carry inside?"

"Thanks." Francesca said, sombrely getting out of the car. "I only have my bag," and leaned inside the vehicle and picked it up off the seat, shut the door and moved forward two steps; then stopped suddenly and turned to faced her friends with tears streaming down her face. "Life just keeps going, as if nothing has happened when someone dies!" she yelled, waving her free arm in the air in a hopeless gesture. "As if nothing has happened – but something DID happen – JULIA DIED! She was a wonderful person. She's left a huge gap in all our lives. I really liked her and enjoyed her company. I just wished I'd told her."

Nicky and Maree were at a loss for words; they had never before seen Francesca so distraught. In an attempt to comfort her, they wrapped their arms around her; but they too ended up weeping.

Rose, who was driving past on her way to the foreshore for her morning walk, saw the trio huddled together and made a sharp U-turn at the lights and swung into the café parking lot, coming to a skidding halt. She flung open her door and ran to her friends.

"What are all of you doing here? Has something else happened?" She asked breathlessly.

Blinking their surprise, the three women wiped their eyes.

"It's alright, Rose. Calm down, sweetie, we're ok." Francesca said, spreading her arms. "Come here," she said, beckoning her to step into the circle, and the others quickly enclosed her too.

"I didn't get the chance to tell Julia how much I admired and appreciated her." Francesca said sincerely, amid the huddle, trying to hold her emotions in check. She smiled at each of them through her tears. "But I can certainly tell you wonderful, crazy ladies – I ..."

"We know, kiddo," Nicky broke in, looking at the others. "We're lucky to have each other. Jules, going like that," she clicked her thumb and finger to emphasise her point, "has made me, and I'm fairly sure I can include all of us when I say, has made me question my own mortality."

Nicky pulled them closer together. "Come on," she said, "hugs and kisses," and Rose yelled, "I'll second that." The four of them giggled and lent forward and pecked one another's cheek. Still encapsulated and savouring the moment, they absent-mindedly began swaying when Nicky quietly hummed *Tennessee Waltz*.

Rose broke ranks and headed for the café with others following behind, laughing at her. "You know I hate that song, Nic." Rose snapped as Nicky skipped alongside of her.

"But I love it. It's nice to dance to. Ah, come on, Rose," she teased. "Don't be a spoil-sport. Look, one, two, three, one, two, three..."

Rose stopped in her tracks when Nicky spun around and came face-to-face with her. She held her breath, as Nicky's bright eyes held hers. Francesca and Maree looked on as they held their breath too, and sighed deeply when Rose beamed the brightest smile and linked arms with her. "Write down the lyrics for me. Ok?"

"Ok." Nicky said grinning, looking over her shoulder, beckoning Francesca and Maree to link up, too and began humming again; Rose shot her eyes upwards in frustration and glanced over at the other two. Nicky winked, turned back to Rose and said, "Get ready for the first lesson: *I was dancin' with my baby, to the Tennessee Waltz, when an old friend I happened to see, introduced her to my loved one, and while they were dancing my friend stole my sweetheart from me ...*" and the others joined in as they swayed up the footpath. "You have a nice voice, Rose." Nicky was saying over the singing.

Within the hour, the Corner Café was brought back to life. One after the other, friends from the village came in, carrying flowers. Sarah was there and even 84-year-old Martin Brown. "We enjoy coming here," he said cheerfully. "It feels homey and all of you feel like family." Francesca glanced over her shoulder at the other three and winked at them.

"Most folk our age," Martin drawled, "become obsolete. It's too much trouble for our families to visit us." He paused, and shook his head, shrugging. "You can't blame them though," he said matter-of-factly, "they have their own lives to deal with, and don't need old folk to be adding to their list of troubles. But," he grinned with a twinkle in his eye, "we don't feel unwanted here, that's why we keep coming back. We listen to, and enjoy all that's going on around here. You gals sure are full of life and fun! And the conversation's stimulating, too. I was here the day you were talking about your trip to Italy." He grinned mischievously. "Now that was an interesting day, I can tell you. Although I didn't agree with what was said about religion and other things, because I'm from the old school; my parents passed on to me their beliefs and I never knew differently. I didn't dare question anything, especially not my priest. But what was said did make me think," he laughed. "But I'm too old to change horses when I'm just about at the end of my ride. I figure when my time comes, God, if he is real, will find me no matter what flavour I am. It's what's in the heart that counts, is my belief."

Francesca looked into his pale, watery eyes, "That's what it's all about, Martin…"

"And we love the songs Nicky plays on the jukebox," he said, interrupting Francesca to avoid further discussion about religion. Francesca understood and remained silent, and listened to him, because she could not ever recall seeing Martin smiling so broadly or having this much to say.

"Did you know," he said without missing a beat, "*Tennessee Waltz* was written in 1946 and was at the top of the country hit charts when I was a young fella? By crikey," he winked, "me and my mate, Carl, thought we were something, waltzing around the dance floor to that tune, Saturday nights at the town hall, with the prettiest girls in town on our arms." His smiled faded and he became serious. "Julia was special – all of you mean a lot to us, love," Martin said, pausing to look around the room. "This place means a lot to all of us, also." When Martin gently laid a large knotted hand on her arm, Francesca covered it with hers. "Thanks love, for thinking of us today," he said, almost choking on his words. "We wanted to – needed to come and pay our respects to Julia. When's the funeral?"

Olivia came up behind Martin and gave him a brief hug, and then faced him, smiling warmly. The others saw her and quickly gathered around. She beamed at everyone.

"There isn't going to be a funeral," Olivia announced, and everyone looked puzzled. "We're celebrating Julia's life tomorrow morning and you're all welcome to join us and, please wear your most colour outfits and happy faces. That's what Julia would have wanted."

Although the chapel was bursting with colour. All, with the exception of Olivia and Ali, wrestled with their emotions. Soft music played as intermittent nose blowing and soft weeping echoed around the crowded chapel. Ben sat forlorn and silent beside Olivia in the front pew, staring at Julia's coffin, while Ali sat the other side of Olivia cradling Angelo, who was sound asleep in her arms.

The congregation wriggled to attention when the vicar came in.

"Today," he began, and then suddenly a brilliant light filled the chapel, enveloping everyone. Faces shone and, instantaneously grief vanished. They all saw and heard Julia amid the light. Her voice sounded like music when she spoke these words; *"Do not stand by my grave and weep. I am not there. I do not sleep. I am a thousand winds that blow. I am the diamond glints on snow. I am the sunlight on ripened grain. I am the gentle autumn rain. When you waken in the morning hush, I am the swift uplifting rush. Of quiet birds in circling flight, I am the soft star-shine at night. Do not stand at my grave and cry...I am not there, I did not die."*

Julia looked pleadingly at Ben and he was instantly transported back to the day she came across that poem, excited to have found it, just weeks before her passing. Her image and the scene were vividly clear in his mind.

"This poem is so beautiful, Ben," she was saying, and began reading it to him.

He was horrified, "but it's about death, Jules."

She smiled into his eyes. "No, no, darling, it's about life. Mary Frye was speaking about eternal life. If ever I..." He kissed her to stop her from saying more. Now he understood what she meant that day.

After the service Ben took Olivia aside. "Mum," he said, "I'm going away – I'm not sure when I'll be back or if I'll ever be back." Olivia looked alarmed. "I'm ok," he reassured her, "I've got a lot to figure out."

On his way out, Ben spoke briefly to Ali. "I want you to know I appreciate everything you're doing for Angelo, for Jules – and, and for me."

Ali nodded, smiling awkwardly about to speak, but Ben hurried away and then hesitated, as if about to say something else, but changed his mind and kept walking. Pasquale observed them from a short distance away. The harnessed jealousy that gnawed constantly at him was beginning once again to stir, hating the way Ali looked at Ben.

32

Life rapidly changed for everyone, especially for Ali, and although friends and family felt nothing would ever be the same without Julia, her apparition inspired them to move forward with renewed hope for the future. Olivia asked Ali to move in with her, and between them they worked out an ideal schedule to care for the baby. Ali loved the child as if he were her own, ignoring Pasquale's jealousy of him.

As the months passed, she could see her relationship with Pasquale was languishing, and did not care. Initially, Ali thought the jealously and temper tantrum were signs that he cared for her. The all-too-frequent temper outbursts became too much for her to cope with. The sanctuary of Olivia's home gave her the opportunity to tell Pasquale that their relationship was not working.

"No, no, Cara mia," he cried, furiously shaking his head and waving his hands in the air, pacing back and forth. "You cannut ta me do dis, we planning togetta future."

Ali looked hopelessly at Pasquale and wondered what it was that she had seen in him. *'He's selfish and demanding. I used to think he was so handsome, but not anymore.'*

As she turned to walk away he grabbed her savagely by the arm. "No Cara, tu sei mio." He shouted at her in Italian as she jerked her arm free.

"No, I'm not yours." She spoke quietly and calmly. "That's where you're wrong. You don't own me. No one owns me, Pasquale. You refuse to accept that, which was your biggest mistake in this relationship." Ali was determined to make her point. "Please don't make this any harder than it has to be. When something is finished – it's finished – we're done," she said, and hurried away, leaving him sobbing and calling to her to come back. When she kept walking and disappeared around the corner, his love for her turned to rage, vowing she would one day pay for breaking his heart.

O'Malley lazily looked up from the lounge when Ali came in and did his usual stretch and roll over, exposing his belly to be scratched.

"How are you goin', big fella?" Ali said, suckered into giving him a belly rub.

"Is that you, Ali?" Olivia called from the bedroom.

"Yeah, I'll be with you in a sec. I'm greeting the lord of the house."

"How did you go with Pasquale?" Olivia asked, coming out of the bedroom carrying Angelo.

"Hi, sweetie," Ali cooed at him and he smiled. "Ok, I guess," she said, looking up at Olivia and screwed up her face, shrugging. "He's Italian. They're passionate and very proud."

"So he's angry and upset?" Olivia replied, raising her brows, and Ali shrugged, "I can handle him, Olivia. Remember, I used to live on the streets," she responded, with mischief in her eyes."

"How could I forget, but that was several years ago. You're a nice girl now." Olivia teased.

Ali raised her brows and with a lopsided grin said, "Gimme the kid," and snatched him from her. As the baby snuggled in to her neck, Ali's voice softened, "It's hard to imagine my past ever existed while holding AJ. It's as if that life never happened. I don't know where I'd be today if you hadn't given me the job. I owe you my life, Olivia."

"You're exactly where you're supposed to be, love, right here. Destiny brought you here, you owe me nothing. We're all winners in this scenario. Especially this little man, he couldn't have a better mother to love him."

"Is that what I am, Olivia? Angelo Jules Rossetti's, mother?"

"Yes, love. It was Julia's wish. I was there, remember?"

"I think Ben will have something to say about that when… when he returns." Ali said, awkwardly.

Olivia wrapped a comforting arm around her, "Oh Ali, you of all people shouldn't worry about Ben. You're very special to him."

"Will he ever come back?"

"Yes, but I'm not sure when that'll be, but I do know when he returns, he'll be ready to move on. I also know how you feel about him."

Ali looked shocked. "I don't know what you mean, Olivia."

"Secret love, indeed. You're so transparent. I've known for a couple of years that you're in love with Ben; perhaps Julia realised it too."

Ali gasped and cursed. "I've never made a play for Ben."

Olivia laughed. "I know. Julia knew it too, that's what makes you trustworthy and special, Ali – not acting on those feelings, only a predatory friend would do that…"

"Julia was my friend. All of you are my friends and my family as well, now. I've never had real friendships before coming to Segal Bay. I'd never betray any of you, I'd leave first." Ali hung her head. "But you're right…about Ben. I've had a crush on him from the first time I saw him, and then I met Jules." She sighed hopelessly. "Even when things looked rocky between them, they were still a solid couple. I could only wish for Ben to love me half as much as he loves Jules."

"No, Ali!" Olivia cut in loud enough to startle Ali and the baby.

"Shhh! It's alright, little man." Ali cooed to him.

"Ooooh, I'm sorry my darling little boy." Olivia said, lowering her voice, gently stroking the baby's head. Once he was settled, she whispered to Ali, "Never, never settle for crumbs from any man, that includes my son! Everyone deserves a one hundred percent from a relationship. Oh, and speaking of family …"

"Were we?"

"Yes, we were. Have you told your parents?"

"No, but I called them and they know I'm ok."

"Hmm, ok then." Olivia smiled with a twinkle in her eye, and then said. "I've got a surprise for you and Francesca."

Ali thought a moment, "What's the occasion? It's not our birthdays."

"No occasion, just a thank you to you both from me. You're both going to the Gold Coast and will be staying overnight at the Versace Resort. I've got tickets to Chef Serge Dansereau of Bathers Pavilion, Master Class; he's promoting his new book and doing cooking demonstrations Saturday afternoon. It sounds wonderful. I'm sure you'll both learn a lot, and have fun as well."

Ali's smile faded, "I don't want to seem ungrateful, Olivia, but what about AJ?"

"Oooh, he'll be fine, the girls will be lining up to take care of him."

"Ok then, it's a date! When do we leave?"

"You can take my car and leave Thursday morning. You should arrive there in plenty of time to do a little shopping, if you like. Francesca mentioned that she needs to get a few things for the nursery.

"That baby's going to be a stunner," Ali grinned, "I saw Jake the day he came looking for Francesca, wow! He's gorgeous, they're both gorgeous."

"Ali!"

"What? There's no harm in admiring. Good on 'em, I say!"

Olivia laughed, "Of course there isn't."

The long journey to the Gold Coast was uneventful. After checking in they were shown to their suite. The opulence of the resort reminded Ali of the lifestyle she once enjoyed, for a brief moment, thought she could easily enjoy it again, and then quickly doused that idea recalling the hefty price she paid for the privilege. *'I will enjoy this'* she thought, with an air of complacency, *'but I certainly won't be seduced by it this time.'*

"Oh my, what a lovely room," Francesca gushed, looking around and then strolling out on to the balcony, "Olivia certainly is generous. Oh my, we must get her a lovely gift before we leave."

"It sure is," Ali replied, hanging up her clothes.

"How are you feeling? Are you up to shopping after a quick bite?" Ali grinned, mischievously raising her eyebrows.

"I'm so excited, I could shop all afternoon," Francesca replied; but Ali cautioned her to take things easy. "I'm studying to be a chef, not a midwife, and you're due in seven weeks, remember?" she said in jest.

They freshened up, ate a light meal and then shopped until the stores closed, returning to the hotel laden down with packages, totally done-in. For a revival treat, Ali suggested a spa, a massage and a facial before dinner.

"You really do know your way around, don't you?" Francesca said with admiration during dinner.

Ali shrugged. "I did a bit of modelling years ago. We were always hanging out in posh places similar to here."

"I can believe that, Ali. You're very beautiful. I'm sure you would've been successful. Why did you stop modelling?"

"I was successful, until I got mixed up with the wrong crowd but really, Francesca, I'm much better off in Segal Bay."

Francesca smiled, "I think we all are, Ali. I couldn't imagine living anywhere else. It was the best decision I made to take Aaron and Michelle on a holiday when Max, my ex-husband walked out on us. I had to get the kids away from the chaos for a while, to take their minds off what was happening. One day, I just told them to pack their bags, we're going to have fun in the sun. I had no idea where we'd go. I just drove and we ended up at Segal Bay. Unfortunately, we had to go back to sell the house. By the time I sold everything to pay Max's debts, there was barely enough money left to get us back to Segal Bay, but we made it and the rest, as they say, is history."

Ali wanted to ask Francesca about the baby and about Jake, but knew if she had wanted her to know, she would have told her. Since Francesca had not mentioned either, Ali did not ask.

The next morning, they both rose early to take advantage of the luxurious pool and spa. As striking women with an air of distinction, everywhere they went heads turned, but neither seemed to notice – Francesca keenly searched her surroundings. From behind sunglasses, her alert eyes darted in every direction looking for Jake, and Ali's mind was AJ.

There was one guest who took particular notice of Ali. He frowned as he tried to recall why she looked familiar and then casually shrugged dismissing her, thinking that all celebrities look alike.

After a leisurely morning, Ali and Francesca made their way down to the terrace for the master class and to meet Chef Serge Dansereau. A few guests were already there, mingling and sipping champagne, chatting among themselves. A waiter welcomed the women as soon as they arrived, offering them a chilled glass of champagne or orange juice from the tray he carried. Ali took champagne and smiled her thanks as Francesca took the juice. While they sipped their drinks and took in their surroundings, admiring the magnificent boats moored at the marina nearby, more guests arrived as Chef Serge joined the group. At the end of the four-hour session, each guest was presented with a copy of his new book, *Seasonal Kitchen*.

"That lunch was so delicious, I can hardly move." Francesca laughed, discreetly rubbing her stomach. "You know, Ali, Olivia will expect us to cook these wonderful dishes for her when we tell her how delicious they are."

"She will, for sure. But I think what'll please her more– her own autographed copy of Serge's book. It's only fitting that Olivia has mine, since she's been a fan of his for years."

"How sweet of you, Ali, Olivia will love it! After we get the books signed, how about we take a stroll to work off the calories we've just gained?"

As they ambled around the shopping mall, the women ruminated about the afternoon, the meal and how personable and friendly Serge was. "I almost feel guilty for enjoying myself so much." Ali admitted.

Francesca's brow creased as she glanced at Ali.

"Well, he's Olivia's favourite chef and ..."

"But that's Olivia," Francesca interrupted "she loves sharing the things she enjoys with the people she cares about – now we love her favourite chef too."

Ali smiled, "Yep, that's Olivia for you. You know," Ali said, with mischief in her voice, "if we leave now, we'd be home by tomorrow evening."

On their way out of the hotel, the arcane guest caught sight of Ali once again; and this time, the sighting jogged his memory as to where he had seen her. 'Aha huh,' he thought, smugly, *'Rhys Ashby's ex. He's offering good money to know her whereabouts.'* The ominous stranger followed the women to their car. He jotted down the number plate and then made a call on his mobile.

Once out of the city, Ali switched on the radio, "I haven't heard the news in ages," she confessed. She listened a few minutes and then switched it off as the newsreader was saying how the southern bushfires were burning out of control. "Ha! Now I remember why I stopped listening to the news. It's full of calamity," she sighed heavily. "I feel so sorry for those poor people suffering the fires, but I'm grateful to be living in Segal Bay, safe and sound in our little piece of heaven!"

33

Olivia was delighted with her autographed copy of Serge's book. She selected a few recipes and added them to the new menu she was preparing. For weeks afterwards, the cookbook and Olivia's new menu were the buzz in the café.

During one of their weekly Skype chats, Olivia was telling Ben about the new menu and how much her friends and customers were enjoying the dishes. Something in Ali snapped when she overheard Ben say that he wished he could have been there. She moved behind Olivia, in view of the screen and, leaning over Olivia's shoulder said, "Well, if you weren't so busy wallowing in self-pity, you could've been and, and what about your son? If you think saying hello to Angelo once a week via Skype is being a father, then you're very wrong – the cats in the cradle, Ben!" Ali declared, before she stormed out of the house, leaving Ben and Olivia staring at each other.

Olivia smiled awkwardly at him, "Well darling, I couldn't have put it better myself. Ali's right."

Ali was enraged. In an effort to release that deep burning rage, she ran top speed along the street to the beach, over the silica sand and halted at the water's edge. Crouched over and gasping for breath, she drew the warm salty air into her lungs, held it, and then exhaled. She did that several times while watching the tide creep in and run along the shore, and then drift back out again, as the rhythm of her heart slowly returned to normal. The moon was big and bright. It cast eerie shadows across the sand. A sudden sense of foreboding sent a chill through her. Ali turned seconds before Rhys smashed her unconscious with the butt of his knife. He stood over her recumbent body, sneering, "I told you, bitch, I'd get you," and then repeatedly kicked her, full force, in tempo with the hateful words he spat out at her.

The vigorous thudding echoing up the street caught Gino's attention who, at the time, was standing outside his restaurant smoking and contemplating tomorrow. He threw the cigarette to the ground, stomped it out and expelled the last of the smoke from his lungs as he gingerly walked in the direction of the sound. From the road, in the moonlight, he saw a man kicking something on the ground.

"Hey!" Gino called, and Rhys Ashby froze a split second, and then turned around. The moonlight shone on his face. Gino recognised him as one of the deadbeat celebrities always in the news.

"Hey, Ashby!" Gino yelled, and pushed his stocky frame forward. Rhys' eyes expanded in terror, darting about, looking for an escape route. He blinked several times, as if waking from sleep, and then ran like the wind in the opposite direction.

Within minutes the street came alive with sirens, flashing lights, locals and tourists. The police took Gino's statement as the ambulance drove away; Ali's injuries were so severe that the doctors were amazed she was still alive; she was in a coma when airlifted to Brisbane.

News of Rhys' arrest and the attack made headlines all over the country. He cowed behind the impeccably dressed Daniel J. Kent when the media frenzy encompassed them as they left the courthouse. Daniel stood tall and unwavering as the gladiator he was, and looked undaunted into the camera and told the media his client was mentally ill and the medication he is taking had affected his rationale, pleading diminished responsibility. Daniel's intonation was steady and believable, and his eyes keen and sharp and truthful, bearing no evidence of the contempt he felt for his client. He was passionate about his profession, and he did his job well.

34

Anton stood in the corner of Ali's dimly lit hospital room, watching over her as she lay connected to tubes and machines. Sounds of early morning city life echoed in the far distance, as the clatter of the hospital waking up penetrated every nerve in Ali's broken body. She stirred. *'I'm alive ... I think.'*

'You are, Ali.' Anton whispered.

Ali's eyes slowly opened, and then widened with surprise. *'I must be dead because I can see you, Anton.'*

'You're in a coma, Ali'

'Am I going to die?'

'I can't tell you that, I don't know but don't be afraid, I'm here for you.'

'It was you in the booth that day, wasn't it?'

Anton nodded. *'You've forgotten that we've met before.'*

'When?'

'You were a child when you, Billy and your parents came to Segal Bay that summer. I had just passed, but you didn't know that. Many times we talked while you played in the sand. You were very protective of your brother, and Ben was protective of you. The three of you were inseparable. Ben hoped to see you the next summer, and then the next. He was very disappointed when you and your family didn't come back.'

'I remember,' Ali said, 'when I stepped out of the coach I... I had this sensation that the place was familiar and this weird snapshot in my head. The boy waving was Ben. I understand the attraction now, and why I kicked my habit so easily. You, Anton, you helped me, didn't you? And you coaxed Jonathan and Harry into doing my makeover too, didn't you?

'None of that's important now, Ali. You've got other business to take care of.'

'Like what?'

'Like fighting for your life. You're not out of the woods yet, not by a long shot.'

Olivia had contacted Elizabeth and Steven before the incident became a *newsflash* on all television channels; they had been in contact with each other since the private investigator, Peter Bates, found Ali. The Swansons caught the first available flight to Brisbane and were soon at Ali's bedside, keeping a vigilant watch over her.

When Ben cleared Customs, he took a taxi from the airport to the hospital. Before the taxi was fully stationary, he threw the driver a fifty dollar note, grabbed his bag, jumped out and rushed up to Ali's room. When he arrived, he hesitated in the doorway. He was depleted and dishevelled and did not recognise the forlorn faces standing by Ali's bed; he only recognised the hopelessness in their eyes.

Olivia came to her son and hugged him, and then gently guided him to Ali's bedside. Ben looked down at her and began to weep.

"Not again. This can't happen again," he said, feeling defeated and dropped into the empty chair beside the bed. When he wrapped his large hands around of Ali's hand, she stirred for the first time. The others quickly moved forward to study Ali, and Ben turned to his mother with hope in his eyes. "That's a good sign, eh?"

Steven called the nurse. She came in, ran a routine check and then left the room without saying a word. The doctor arrived shortly afterwards and examined Ali. He turned to the group and smiled. The only words Ben absorbed of the conversation was the doctor said, *"It was hopeful."*

The mood in the room lightened. Olivia took that opportunity to introduced Ben to Elizabeth and Steven.

"You've certainly grown into a handsome young man, Ben." Elizabeth said, offering her hand.

Ben hesitated, and gave his mother a puzzled look.

Olivia smiled. "You were a boy when Elizabeth and her family visited Segal Bay. I had forgotten about it until Elizabeth mentioned they spent a summer there."

Ben's eyes lit up. "Do you have a son named Billy?"

"Yes," Steven replied, and Ben grinned.

"Now that Ali's in good hands, I must get back to the Bay," Olivia said, and kissed Ali on the forehead and whispered, "Get well soon, darling, we all need and love you."

Ben booked into a hotel near the hospital so he could be with Ali, returning to the hotel only to shower and change. Every day he talked and read to Ali, and then began pleading with her to come back.

"This is my fault," he sobbed. "You wouldn't be lying here if I'd been home looking after Angelo. You were right to be angry with me, Ali. I was selfish. I'm so sorry, please forgive me. I can't promise you anything, there's no certainty in promises because...because I'm not in control of our destiny. All I, we can hope for is one day at a time. The one thing I am very certain of is that I love you. I have from the first time we met, way back when we were children. Every summer I hoped you'd come back. Please wake up! "

Ali opened her eyes and tried to talk. Ben looked up at her when she moved. "Wait! Wait, Ali. I'll call someone, er, the doctor," Ben said, in a whirl of excitement and uncertainty of leaving her alone; and then decided to just dash out to the hallway and call the nurse.

A few hours later, Ali was fully conscious and propped up in bed, talking to Ben through a lopsided mouth. Most of the swelling had subsided; the bruising was still visible and fading into a yellowish green. When Ali caught sight of her image in the mirror, and tried to laugh, she groaned as a twinge of pain shot through her jaw. Ben overreacted and began fussing, asking if she was ok. Ali lifted her hand to indicate she was.

"Take it easy," she mumbled. "I'm ok. Really."

Ben apologised and sat back in the chair, searching for the right words to tell Ali how he felt.

"Thanks, Ben really, I mean it." Ali paused. "We have to talk," she said looking, perplexed. "This, you and me could be an illusion. We were children when we met." She made a sound like a laugh. "We're strangers who like well, in a way, love each other. The reality is Ben, we don't know each other like this. Well, you know what I mean and, and another thing is," Ali said, looking down at his hand, "you're still wearing your wedding ring."

Ben nodded, realising he must show Ali how he felt, and slowly backed out of the room. "I'll be back soon," he said, and disappeared around the corner, leaving Ali totally bewildered.

Several hours later, Ben returned with a huge bunch of long-stemmed yellow roses, and a gift-box tied with a big yellow satin ribbon. Ali's eyes lit up when he handed them to her; she also noticed he was not wearing the wedding ring.

"What's this for?"

"The yellow roses represent our friendship. The next bunch I give you will be pink, to mark the beginning of our love, and when the time is right, red roses, ok? Ali nodded; afraid she was still in a coma.

"And since you can't get out and buy a new dress for our first date tonight, I bought you something to wear. Open the box."

Ali pinched herself on the arm just to make sure she was conscious, and smiled as best as her injuries would allow while undoing the ribbon, removed the lid and peeled back the tissue paper. She gasped, "It's beautiful," and lifted out a long ivory, silk nightdress.

"Good, you like it!" He smiled, feeling very satisfied with himself. "I've got a few things to do, so go get prettied up, I'll be back as soon as I can."

That night, and the nights following, Ben got permission to have candlelit dinners with Ali in her room, during which time they got to know each other, sharing the good and the not-so-good details of their past. At the end of the week, Ben presented Ali with a dozen red roses and a diamond ring. Ali recognised the ring; it was his mother's precious engagement ring. Olivia was giving them her blessing.

"Well," Ben said, "I don't need any more time, I know how I feel and it's no illusion that I love you. Marry me, Ali?"

"I thought you'd never ask." She teased, "Gimme that ring!" and he gently slid the ring onto her finger. They looked at each other and smiled, both thinking how wonderfully surreal life is, meeting as children and now, years later, engaged to be married.

"I love you, Ben." Ali said, gently kissing him, "And I'm ok with the love and the life you and Jules shared. We all loved her, and she's Angelo's mum so, when something reminds you of her, it's ok."

"It's all good, Ali. I get what you're saying. I've said my goodbyes and, yes, I know there will be times, but that's ok… you're so generous, so kind and so very understanding – there're just some of the reasons why I love you."

35

Francesca's mobile began ringing. She shoved her hand deep into her bag, frantically fumbling around, looking for the phone.

"Damn it!" She cursed softly, "I can never find anything in here when I need to."

"Perhaps you need small bag."

Francesca spun around, "Marco!" she exclaimed, delighted to see him.

"When did you arrive?"

"I get early fight, and then get car," he shrugged, "no matter–I here now," he beamed. They embraced and pecked at each other's cheeks, European style.

"Aah, I see you glow with child, like the Madonna."

Looping her arm through his, she laughed, "Still charming as ever, I see. Come on, I want to you meet Olivia."

Anton stood at the window. He was smiling. Olivia saw him and wondered what made him smile. She was about to investigate, when Francesca came in with a very attractive man on her arm. Olivia thought he looked familiar and then realised it was Marco, the man she had seen many times in Francesca's photographs of Italy.

"I hope you're not planning to go anywhere today, Olivia." Francesca said, rushing up to her. "Marco's here. I'm hoping you'd have time to show him around."

Olivia, who was never one for playing games, smiled sweetly at Marco, and then flashed Francesca a mock–annoyed look. "I'd be delighted, Marco, but I do believe this sightseeing trip is a setup, something Francesca has planned for us to get acquainted. So if you're fine with that, then so am I."

"I delight with, as you say, setup. It pleasure and great honour," he bowed.

Olivia smiled, "Well I guess we can chat over lunch. Have you eaten?" she asked, as she led him to the corner booth. "How was your stay in Sydney? Did you manage to get in some sightseeing?"

Francesca was busy behind the counter when the room went silent. Everyone, with the exception of a small group of tourists, chatting among themselves in the corner booth, waited with great expectation when they saw Jake standing at the door, watching Francesca. She looked up and gasped.

"Francesca," he said, loud enough for all to hear, slowly walking towards her.

"I will say this just once and, if you refuse me, I will leave and never bother you ever again: Will you marry me? I want to spend the rest of my life with you. You're more important to me than anything or anyone."

Francesca took a deep breath and nervously placed the cup she was holding on the shelf and stepped out from behind the counter.

"Yes," she said softly, choking back joyful tears.

The whole place burst into applause as it was Jake's turn to be surprised.

"When? How?" he muttered, looking at Francesca's swollen belly.

Someone shouted, "If you don't know how mate, then you'd better go back to school," and the room rocked with laughter.

Ignoring the comment and everybody in the room, Jake reached for Francesca and kissed her. Francesca whispered, "You'd better marry me very soon, our daughter is due any day now."

Olivia came up behind them and whispered. "Perhaps you two should go home."

"I can't leave you with a full house." Francesca protested. Marco was beside Olivia in a flash and chipped in.

"Olivia not alone, I here. I help. My papa once had busy ristorante in my country, I help many times." He said proudly, offering his hand to Jake, "I Marco, you Jake, yes?"

"That's right." Jake grinned, shaking Marco's hand. "It's good to finally meet you, Marco. Francesca speaks highly of you and thanks for taking good care of her in Italy."

Marco smiled and bowed slightly, "The pleasure mine."

Jake took hold of Francesca's arm and slowly backed away. "Thanks Marco, for filling in for Francesca. I owe you one. Come on girl, we've a lot to discuss."

On their way home, Jake asked Francesca why she had not contacted him about the baby. "I had no idea where to find you."

"I left all my details in the book you were reading, just in case you changed your mind."

"I was devastated when you left, I've not looked at that book since, it's still on the bedside table. I kept working so I wouldn't have time to think, but none of that's important now. You're here."

She looked up at him, puzzled, as they walked over to her car. "What made you come back?"

"Something my father said to me years ago."

"What was that?"

"I was a kid at the time, curious about girls and things. I asked him how he knew Mum was the right person for him. He's Australian and she's African-American. He told me they kept crossing paths – first in London, where she was studying law and then, a few years later, in New York when he was visiting friends. As it turned out, they had mutual friends there. Dad was a few years older than Mum and already established as an architect. He said that although they had met only briefly, he could not erase her from his mind and that was when he knew she was *the one*. He went back to America and proposed to her. I couldn't get you from my mind, either, and so I had to come back and try one more time."

36

Nature was at its best on the day of the wedding, giving its seal of approval to the nuptial. The sun's golden rays hit the earth and sent a kaleidoscope of colour through flowering shrubs around the Bay. A fusion of colour from the cobalt sky was reflected in crisp white capped waves, running along the pristine silica sand, and a robust frangipani scent floated along the beach. Even turf along the foreshore seemed lusher and greener. An intoxicating excitement filled the air.

Everyone was present, with the exception of Ali and Ben who were watching the ceremony via Madison's video phone.

The bridegroom, tall and broad-shouldered waited for his bride on the lush green, at the top of the meandering foreshore, by the canopy covered in tiny white roses – where they would soon pledge their love to one another. Maddie mingled through the guests, carrying her mobile, so they could speak to Ali and send her their best wishes. Ali and Ben sat together on the bed with Angelo, chatting, laughing and waving to everyone. An animated hush gripped the crowd when they sighted the limousine. A voice, coloured with excitement, came through the mobile shouting, "She's coming!"

All heads turned when Francesca draped in flowing cream silk and georgette, nervously clutching her bouquet of red-wine and champagne roses stepped from the vehicle escorted by Aaron and Michelle. The string quartet began to play *Ave Maria*, and the smiling trio slowly walked along the carpet, to meet Jake. Francesca looked Maddie's way and saw Ali and Ben's smiling images on the mobile and she waved to them.

As Michelle walked beside her mother, she scanned the crowd looking for Hanna. The girls had been inseparable since high school. Michelle released a little sigh when she saw Hanna a little farther up the front, standing with Olivia. Hanna gave Michelle a little wave. Olivia smiled, thinking it was wonderful that their relationship was long-lasting.

A burst of applause, cheers and laughter echoed in the air, and doves took flight when the celebrant announced Jake and Francesca, "husband and wife!" They both turned around, full of smiles when suddenly Francesca's smile faded with the intensity of a sudden pain in her back. She was hunched over looking at Jake. "It's time!" she said, struggling to remain calm. "Our daughter's coming!"

Aaron, Michelle and Hanna followed the ambulance to the hospital in a borrowed car. They did not have a long arduous wait for the baby's arrival, she was born at the hospital's entrance.

****

A year later, family and friends gathered once again at the Corner Café, this time to celebrate Christmas. Olivia was putting the finishing touches to the decorations when Anton appeared beside her.

"It's time for me to leave, my darling," he whispered. "Marco's a good man. He will look after you. He's already in love with you."

"When will I see you again?" she asked Anton, but he had already vanished.

"When you like, Olivia," Marco replied, coming from the kitchen. "I thinking of living here, is good for you?"

Olivia spun around when Marco spoke. She smiled warmly and linked her arm in his. "Yes, it's good for me, Marco." She said, "That way we can really get to know each other." He gently patted her hand and then released it, and then went over to the jukebox. "You 'ave Italian love song, *Al Di La*. This very beautiful romantic song. I play. We dance?" Olivia nodded. Marco slipped the coin in the machine and chose the song – a full orchestra with violins and piano played as Connie Frances' voice echoed around the room, and they danced.

The couple were so engrossed in the moment that neither noticed they had an audience. An ear-splitting applause and cheers filled the room when the song finished. Marco smiled and ceremoniously bowed, and then proudly led Olivia by the hand to the table. He pulled out a chair and she sat down beside Sarah Connelly. Francesca, Jake carrying little Matilda, and Arron, Michelle and Hanna quickly joined her, followed by Madison and her parents, Lilly and Rob Weston.

Olivia looked up at the wall clock just as Maree, Rose and Nicky, laden down with food, wine and gifts burst through the door. They were laughing and playfully teasing their partners, Greg, Joe and Carl, and by the ruckus they made they had already begun to celebrate. "Hey, everyone," Nicky shouted, "Merry Christmas, looks like the gang's all here" and everyone shouted back, "Merry Christmas!"

"Not yet, Nic," Olivia said. "Ben, Ali and Angelo haven't arrived yet, neither has Elizabeth and Steven … nor Gino, he said he'd drop by for a while."

"Yes, we have." Ben said, coming through the door, followed by the others.

While Ali, her friends and her family celebrated, Rhys Ashby was festering away in his room at *Beckon House*, a mental institution for the criminally insane, waiting for the staff to leave for their midday meal. They had done the last of their rounds and would not be back for another four hours, just enough time for him to make his escape.

Katie, Lilly's assistant, was driving home from her parents' house when a news flash interrupted the program she was listening to on her car radio. She almost skidded onto the shoulder of the road, turning the car in the direction of the café. She came to a screaming halt and ran into the café, shouting, "Rhys Ashby's escaped!" and the room went deadly quiet. Gino excused himself and went outside. He calmly took out his mobile, dialled a number, waited a moment and then said, "I need a cleaner."

Acknowledgements

My heartfelt thanks must go to Jodie Wood, Erin Flux, Jenny Mansell-Black and Elaine West for their most valued assistance in the preparation on this book. Thank you so very much!

To my sister Lynne West for her enthusiam and support of my work: to my youngest daughter Christy, my confidant, my best friend, my rock.

www.ingramcontent.com/pod-product-compliance
Lightning Source LLC
Chambersburg PA
CBHW052022290426
44112CB00014B/2336